A HISTORY OF
CANNON MOUNTAIN

Trails, Tales and Skiing Legends

MEGHAN McCARTHY McPHAUL

Charleston

THE
History
PRESS

D1262061

Published by The History Press
Charleston, SC 29403
www.historypress.net

Front cover, top: New England Ski Museum photo. *Bottom*: Meghan McCarthy McPhaul
photo, 2011.

Back cover, top left: Meghan McCarthy McPhaul photo. *Top right*: New England Ski
Museum photo. *Other*: Hochgebirger Carolyn Beckedorff. *Photo by Paul Hayes/
Record-Littleton.*

First published 2011

Manufactured in the United States

ISBN 978.1.60949.043.0

Library of Congress Cataloging-in-Publication Data

McPhaul, Meghan McCarthy.
A history of Cannon Mountain : trails, tales, and skiing legends / Meghan McCarthy
McPhaul.
p. cm.
Includes bibliographical references.
ISBN 978-1-60949-043-0
1. Downhill skiing--New Hampshire--Cannon Mountain--History. 2. Trails--New
Hampshire--Cannon Mountain--History. 3. Ski resorts--New Hampshire--Cannon
Mountain--History. 4. Skiers--New Hampshire--Cannon Mountain--Biography.
5. Cannon Mountain (N.H.)--Biography. 6. Mountain life--New Hampshire--
Cannon Mountain--History. 7. Cannon Mountain (N.H.)--Social life and customs.
I. Title.
GV854.5.N4M38 2011
796.93'509742--dc22
2011015495

To Kathy Keegan and Red McCarthy, who met on Cannon Mountain's Middle Hardscrabble trail in 1969 and raised a family of Cannon skiers.

And to all the people who have worked and skied at Cannon and consider the mountain home.

CONTENTS

CONTENTS

Introduction

SKIING COMES TO FRANCONIA

The story of skiing at Cannon Mountain weaves a winding trail. It begins with the area's early foray into mountain tourism, meanders past a grand old inn and rustic ski lodges, traverses the slopes and pitches of a forested granite dome and schusses downhill on the exhilaration of generations of skiers. It reaches beyond the trails of Cannon to include Swiss and Austrian skiers, Bostonians, Olympians and longtime residents of the Franconia region whose families have worked and skied at Cannon for decades.

From Cannon's earliest days as a ski center, it has been known as a "skier's mountain," a place both challenging and unpretentious. "Although they aren't all togged up in the fanciest and latest of ski ensembles with brilliant colored jackets and loud shirts, the skiers who run the trails on Cannon Mountain…are better than average; you have to be to dash down the lightning-fast tracks all around the mountain and still keep control," wrote one observer in 1941. "Up here, they go in more for ability and stamina than they do for flashy costumes."[1] The same is true seventy years later.

Cannon is unique among modern ski areas in other ways as well. The mountain is owned by the State of New Hampshire, which has posed different management challenges from those encountered at privately owned ski areas. The managers at Cannon have to answer to a legislature of more than four hundred members, and most of the legislators are not experts on ski area operations. Cannon is also part of Franconia Notch State Park, surrounded by state and national forest land, and so is not enveloped by

View of Franconia Notch, circa 1900, looking south with Franconia Village in the foreground. Mount Lafayette is on the left, with Cannon Mountain on the right. *Library of Congress, Prints & Photographs Division, LC-USZ62-123131.*

endless rows of condominiums and other developments, which is either a pristine blessing or a commercialistic curse, depending on your perspective.

Created by fire and ice, Franconia Notch is filled with natural wonders and magnificent scenery. Cannon was formed from molten magma some 200 million years ago and exposed by the forces of weather and erosion over millions of years. Ice Age glaciers carved the deep U-shaped Notch, and weathering and erosion from the melting ice left behind such marvels as the Old Man of the Mountain, the Flume Gorge and the Basin.[2] The mountain takes its name from another rock formation, resembling a cannon, near the summit. Weather remains a dominant feature at Cannon, as scouring winds push fiercely through the Notch. A 1973 gust of more than 199.5 miles per hour recorded on Cannon's summit was then the third-highest measured wind speed in the world.[3]

Since the 1930s, skiing and Cannon Mountain have been part of the economy, heritage and very landscape of Franconia. The mountain hamlet was settled in the late 1700s, when its first hardy residents logged

Cannon Mountain is named after this rock formation, resembling a cannon, which sits on the southeast shoulder of the mountain. *Postcard, copyright Roland E. Peabody, 1941. Courtesy Dick Hamilton.*

the thick forests and picked endless stones from the fields to create farms. The discovery of two veins of iron ore near the village around the turn of the nineteenth century created a new industry, as the ore was smelted and crafted into wrought-iron tools or exported from town via horse-drawn wagon. The discovery of the famous Old Man of the Mountain in 1805 and the mid-nineteenth-century dawning of the era of grand hotels built in the mountains thrust Franconia into the tourism business.

The Old Man, that huge granite profile gazing from the edge of Cannon Mountain over Franconia Notch, drew curious visitors, myriad vacationers and renowned writers from the time of its discovery by surveyors until it tumbled from its perch in 2003. Word of the Old Man and of Franconia's beauty spread, and soon hotels were established in and near the Notch, capped by the grandest of all: the Profile House.

Built on the floor of the Notch in 1852 by Richard Taft, the Profile House thrived through seven decades of summer visitors, as city dwellers arrived seeking the clean air and wild wonders of the North Country. But on August 3, 1923, the Profile House met the fate of so many grand hotels of the era when the entire complex burned to the ground in a matter of hours. The Abbott family, who had purchased the Profile House only two years before, put the entire Franconia Notch property up for sale, with a $400,000

The Old Man of
the Mountain. *Dick
Hamilton photo.*

price tag. The property comprised some six thousand acres of wilderness, including Cannon Mountain.

Faced with losing to the lumber industry the natural wonders that had drawn so many to the region for so long, area residents and those from afar banded together in an incredible effort, led by the Society for the Protection of New Hampshire Forests, to protect Franconia Notch. More than fifteen thousand individuals contributed funds to help the state purchase the property, and in September 1928, the Franconia Notch Forest Reservation and Memorial Park was dedicated to New Hampshire citizens who have served the country in times of war.[4]

The preservation of Franconia Notch as a state park correlated with the emergence of the sport of skiing in America. Adventure seekers, mainly college students and members of outing clubs, were beginning to explore snowy hills on long wooden skis. In New Hampshire, not far from Franconia, the Dartmouth Outing Club organized ski races in the late 1920s. Closer to

The Profile House complex, circa 1901. The Cannon Mountain Aerial Tramway now runs adjacent to the ridgeline, seen behind the hotel in this postcard image. *Library of Congress, Prints & Photographs Division, Detroit Publishing Company Collection, LC-D4-13992.*

home, in 1929, an entrepreneurial young woman created the first resort-based ski school in North America at her family's inn, just up the road from the village of Franconia. In 1931, the first snow train, run by the Boston & Maine Railroad, carried some two hundred snow enthusiasts from Boston to the snow country of New Hampshire. These trains, complete with ski tuning cars and ski instructors, were an instant hit. From 1931 to the start of World War II, the Boston & Maine snow trains carried more than a quarter of a million passengers to the winter wonderland of the North Country.[5] Rope tows, powered by car or tractor engines, began popping up in pastures throughout the region during the mid-1930s.

Franconia emerged as an early leader in American skiing, transforming the local hospitality business from a summer industry into a year-round commerce. The first trail cut for down-mountain skiing was carved from the forests on Cannon Mountain. The first passenger aerial tramway in North America was built here, the first professional ski patrol in the country was established at Cannon and the first World Cup races on the continent were contested on the mountain. Cannon Mountain is home hill to two of

View of Franconia Notch looking south from Franconia in 2011. *Author photo.*

the country's oldest ski clubs, and more than a dozen members of the U.S. National Ski Hall of Fame have long-standing ties to skiing in Franconia.

The ski area has passed through glory days and tough times, and with the evolution of the sport and the creation of ski areas all over the country, Cannon no longer stands alone at the apex of American skiing. But the skiing legacy is as strong as ever on Cannon's slopes, where you'll sometimes find an Olympic racer or two, skiers seeking the adventure of hidden trails stashed in the secret folds of the forest and die-hards who have descended the mountain for a half century or more. And always, come powder snow or Cannon's famous icy winds, the pure delight of sliding downhill that began with the pioneers of American skiing echoes in the happy whoops of today's skiers and the graceful arc of skis carving down winding trails that are both novel and timeless.

PECKETT'S-ON-SUGAR HILL

Kate Peckett, Sig Buchmayr and Ski Beginnings

In many ways, the story of skiing at Cannon Mountain begins with Peckett's-on-Sugar Hill. A farmhouse-turned-classy-inn located just up the road from Franconia village, with a breathtaking view of the magnificent peaks of the Franconia Range and a fashionable class of clientele, Peckett's began catering to snow lovers at the turn of the twentieth century. Winter guests enjoyed such chilly thrills as tobogganing, snowshoeing, ice-skating and horse-drawn sleigh rides, as well as meals cooked and served outdoors. In 1929, when most other area inns and hotels remained closed during the snowy months, Peckett's began offering ski instruction to guests, establishing the first resort-based ski school in North America and bringing the skiing boom to Franconia. The skiing venture at Peckett's was led by Katharine "Kate" Peckett, youngest daughter of the inn's proprietors. The reach of Kate Peckett and the ski school at the grand Sugar Hill inn extended to the very heart of an emerging American ski culture.

Peckett's-on-Sugar Hill began as a modest farmhouse and grew into "a mellow, rambling, beautifully-run inn…[and] one of the choicest resorts in the East."[6] Proprietors Robert and Katharine Peckett—affectionately called Father and Mother Peckett by both guests and employees—added various wings to the original structure and built "cottages" nearby to accommodate more guests. The Pecketts lived in the hotel, took their meals in the elegant dining room and created an atmosphere that was simultaneously refined and unpretentious. Mother Peckett held court from her living room next to the front desk—there was no lobby—keeping track of all comings and goings

Katharine and Robert Peckett entertaining a guest's dog. *Sugar Hill Historical Museum.*

and making everyone feel at home. Father Peckett spent evenings peeling chestnuts by a roaring fire of birch logs and chatting with guests.[7]

From these cozy confines, guests explored the outdoors in all seasons. During the summer, they could play the nine-hole pitch-and-putt golf course that ran along either side of the elaborate gardens. There were outings—summer and winter—to "camps" in the mountains. Those less adventurous could simply relax in the yard and take in the view or select a book from the shelves of Peckett's charming library set on a hillside nearby.

Peckett's defied classification—not large enough to be a grand hotel, yet far classier than a standard country inn—and attracted as patrons leaders of commerce, politics, theater and screen. Presidents Calvin Coolidge and Herbert Hoover stayed there, as did Eleanor Roosevelt and Supreme Court chief justices Charles Evans Hughes and Harlan Fiske Stone. Hollywood stars Margaret Sullivan and Bette Davis, who made Sugar Hill her second home, lodged at Peckett's, along with Helen Keller, Dr. Charles Mayo and countless others.[8] With Peckett's focus on skiing, the notable list of patrons grew to include promoters of a fledgling American sport who would have great influence on skiing both locally and nationally.

Kate Peckett embarked on her ski school endeavor after skiing at Engelberg, Switzerland, during a 1928 visit while she was completing a cooking course in Paris. She was so impressed by the European ski schools that she enticed her parents to visit that winter and then persuaded them to allow her to start a ski school at Peckett's. The twenty-three-year-old Kate returned to Sugar Hill to oversee the clearing of a slope adjacent to the grand inn. She hired two German instructors to teach skiing to Peckett's guests during the winter of 1929–30[9] and promoted skiing to the "big car jet set" of the era.[10]

It wasn't only the rich and famous, however, who learned to slide downhill at Peckett's. Many local residents also discovered the sport there, including Roland Peabody and his son, Roger, who would later become the first two managers of the Cannon Mountain Aerial Tramway. Local youngsters honed their schussing skills at Peckett's at a time when skiing was being discovered around New England. These young skiers included Norwood Ball, Roger Peabody, Bertram Herbert and Bobby Clark, who began skiing at Peckett's as grade schoolers and soon became junior assistants to the instructors there. A few years later, they were the core of a powerful racing team at Franconia's Dow Academy.

Local children often mixed with Peckett's guests on the ski slopes and at the popular afternoon tea served by Mother Peckett. "I remember this being a real elegant, old-fashioned type hotel. And…there'd be guests from the hotel and there'd be area people," Ball said in a 1979 interview. "At first, being sort of unused and unaccustomed to that society, I was a little apprehensive. But Mrs. Peckett made you feel right at home and always had some questions to ask about your family…So pretty soon we thought nothing about it, and we'd be talking to the guests and really having a ball, same as they were."[11]

The charm of Peckett's ski school increased exponentially when Austrian Sig Buchmayr joined the staff as an instructor during the school's second winter. Buchmayr became ski director in 1931, a position he held until Peckett's closed its winter operations in 1939. He was "energetic, engaging and dedicated to the sport."[12] Just over five feet tall, Buchmayr was larger than life, as charismatic as he was athletic. In 1933, a writer from the *New Yorker* described him as "a congenial and diminutive young Austrian jack rabbit…[whose] skis are as much a part of him as his socks."[13]

Left: Kate Peckett and Sig Buchmayr at Peckett's-on-Sugar Hill in the 1930s. *New England Ski Museum (NESM) Collection.*

Below: A class at Peckett's warms up for its lesson in front of the inn. *NESM Collection.*

Buchmayr entertained Peckett's guests with handstands, somersaults, yodeling and stories, often while decked out in lederhosen. Like any reputable ski professional of the era, however, Buchmayr was serious about skiing. Before heading down the slopes at Peckett's—and, in later years, to ski the Taft Trail at Cannon—he and the other instructors led students through a rigorous warm-up of calisthenics. Rope tows soon became a popular means of uphill transportation for skiers, but there would be no such contraption at Peckett's, since Sig deemed them "detrimental to good ski-ing" and believed that skiers "must be able to climb in order to excel in the sport."[14]

There was more to skiing at Peckett's-on-Sugar Hill than the act of sliding downhill. The Pecketts created a "Sonnenstate," or ice palace, from large blocks of ice stacked into walls to shield sunbathers on fur-covered deckchairs from the wind. The ice was cut from a nearby pond and transported uphill for this luxury. After dark, winter guests were invited to gather in the "Stube," where supper was served buffet style, and many visitors donned Tyrolean costumes. "Ringing with song, laughter and conversation carried on in several languages, the atmosphere [was] distinctly foreign and the room most popular," and if some unlucky guest arrived without a dirndl or lederhosen, he or she could visit the Peckett's shop, featuring items from the upscale B. Altman department store of New York City.[15]

A group of female skiers, still wearing boots, soaks up the sun in the Sonnestate at Peckett's. *Sugar Hill Historical Museum.*

Through B. Altman & Co., Kate Peckett influenced not only the sport of skiing but its fashions as well. In the mid-1930s, she became a buyer for the store's new ski shops, traveling to European ski centers to bring back the latest and greatest fabrics and styles. B. Altman touted her as the "foremost authority on ski-ing and ski clothes in America,"[16] and Peckett had her own label at the store.

With Kate's insight into skiing and her parents' support of the venture, Peckett's became the gathering place of skiing greats and those who would shape the sport in Franconia and throughout the country. The Hochgebirge ski club, comprising wealthy Bostonians, frequented Peckett's. Hochgebirger Alexander Bright was a key proponent in building an aerial tramway on Cannon Mountain, an idea he broached in 1933 and one that Kate Peckett and her parents supported. Charles "Minnie" Dole, who founded the National Ski Patrol and helped form the fabled 10th Mountain Division during World War II, skied at Peckett's. So did the popular radio personality Lowell Thomas, who promoted skiing in part by broadcasting live from ski centers around the country.

As skiing gained popularity and its followers became more proficient, Kate Peckett looked beyond the sloping fields near her family's hotel for

A crowd gathers to watch a race at Peckett's slope in the late 1930s. Cannon and Mount Jackson are in the center background, with the Richard Taft Trail visible at the left of Mount Jackson and the thirteen turns of the Tucker Brook Trail barely visible down the right side of the mountain. *NESM Collection*.

more challenging ski terrain. Her gaze turned across the valley to Cannon Mountain, and she set to work raising funds for what would become the imposing and thrilling Richard Taft Trail. Kate Peckett and her father, in 1933, were also among the founders of the Franconia Ski Club, which did much to promote skiing and the region.

For the critical role she played in developing American skiing, Kate Peckett—by then Katharine Peckett Holman—was inducted into the U.S. National Ski Hall of Fame in 1982. Several of the skiers associated with Peckett's-on-Sugar Hill are there, too: Dole, Thomas, Peckett's instructors Otto Lang and Sig Buchmayr, Roland and Roger Peabody and Alec Bright. As skiing developed as a sport and an industry, more inns and hotels in the region began catering to skiers. Peckett's closed its doors to winter guests in 1939 but remained a summer operation. In 1952, Kate's nephew, Ross Coffin, purchased Peckett's-on-Sugar Hill from his grandfather. Coffin maintained the high standards of Peckett's and was a strong supporter of skiing in the area, becoming a devoted booster of the Franconia Ski Club.

In 1967, Peckett's-on-Sugar Hill closed for good, and the grand inn that stood on the hill overlooking the White Mountains was razed in 1969.[17] The ski slope cleared in 1929 to serve Kate Peckett's vision of winter recreation has reverted to dense forest. Kate Peckett died in 1999, and most of the skiers who learned the sport at Peckett's are gone now, too. But their influence on skiing reaches across the decades, lingering in the smooth glide of skis down mountain slopes and in the exhilaration of generations of skiers who have reveled in the sport.

THE RICHARD TAFT TRAIL

The Advent of Down-Mountain Skiing

The Richard Taft Trail inspired awed conversation around ski lodge tables and on snow trains from Boston as soon as it was carved from the dense forest on the north shoulder of Cannon Mountain. The Taft, with its precipitous pitch and narrow corners, was the first trail in New England cut specifically for down-mountain skiing. Construction began with local funds and labor in 1932 and was completed the following year by the Depression-era Civilian Conservation Corps. Even before its completion, the Taft earned a reputation as a serious test of skiing prowess.

"The broad but murderous Richard Taft Trail, slashed out of the timber on the steep side of Cannon Mountain, will probably become famous when it is finished," predicted one visitor to Peckett's in 1933. "So far, only a couple of miles have been cleared; but if you can stand at the foot of that run—let alone at the top—without breaking into a sweat of fear and catching your death of cold, you're either an ignoramus or an Alpine expert."[18]

The Taft came into being as skiing's popularity blossomed throughout the region and skiers sought more challenging terrain than the open pastures and mountain carriage roads then available for skiing. In Franconia, Kate Peckett and other skiers looked to Cannon Mountain and envisioned a ski run a bit steeper, a bit longer and a bit more adventuresome than the relatively tame slope at Peckett's. Kate organized a local fundraising effort to develop such a trail. To design it, she enlisted Peckett's instructor Duke Dimitri von Leuchtenberg, a descendant of Russia's Nicholas I and cousin to the Romanoff czars, who found his way to the United States in the 1930s.[19]

The racing portion of the Richard Taft Trail, as seen from Bald Nob in Franconia Notch State Park. Part of the trail would later be incorporated into the Mittersill ski area. *NESM Collection.*

The Richard Taft Trail consisted of two distinct sections. One would become known as Taft Slalom, reaching down in a relatively straight track from the summit of Cannon Mountain. The second section of the trail began at the top of Mount Jackson (later developed as the Mittersill ski area)—a short climb up the "saddle" from the bottom of the slalom run. Dubbed the Taft Race Trail, it plunged in tight curves through hardwood forest, careening around sharp corners and down steep pitches to its conclusion near the present-day entrance to Mittersill on Route 18. When completed, the Taft stretched nearly two miles from the top of Cannon to the end of the race trail, varying in width from fifteen feet to sixty feet, with a vertical drop of eighteen hundred feet.[20] Although the Taft Race Trail is mostly reverted to forest now, Taft Slalom remains part of Cannon's trail network.

Richard Taft, proprietor of the Profile House in Franconia Notch, for whom the famous Taft Trail was named. *Franconia Heritage Museum.*

Mother Peckett named the Richard Taft Trail after the man who had built the grand Profile House in Franconia Notch in 1852.[21] It is unlikely that Richard Taft, who died in 1881, ever skied, and it's unknown how he would have perceived such a sport. But he brought the era of grand hotels and mountain tourism to Franconia and did much to promote the area and preserve its natural beauty. At the height of its grandeur, the Profile House contained four hundred rooms, with some thirty guest cottages surrounding the hotel. Guests enjoyed lawn tennis, a private golf course, fishing and boating on Echo and Profile lakes and hiking or riding burros to such heights as the summit of Mount Lafayette. Perhaps the most famous visitor to the Profile House was President Ulysses S. Grant, who came north in 1869, only a few years after the end of the Civil War.[22]

After the Profile House was destroyed by fire in 1923, the State of New Hampshire purchased the six thousand acres surrounding the site to create what is now Franconia Notch State Park. The Richard Taft Trail was constructed on property owned partly by the state and partly by Taft's heirs.[23] The Valley Station of the Cannon Mountain Aerial Tramway sits roughly where the Profile House once stood.

The Taft Trail, however, was cut five years before the tram arrived and on the opposite side of Cannon Mountain. Creating a mountain ski

Workers clear the Taft Trail in 1933. The trail in the background leads from the bottom of Taft Slalom on Cannon over the saddle to the Taft Race Trail on Mount Jackson. *NESM Collection.*

trail was a huge undertaking in those early days of skiing, decades before snowmaking or trail grooming equipment. Trail builders sought northerly exposure to prevent snow from excessive melting and subsequent crusting. Narrow, winding trails offered further protection from wind. Crews of men armed with axes, crowbars and dynamite—there were no chainsaws or bulldozers then—cleared the trails of trees and pulled stumps and rocks from the ground.

Although local laborers began work on the Taft in the summer of 1932, less than half the trail was cut by that winter. It seems serendipitous, then, that in 1933 the New Hampshire State Development Commission formed a Ski Trails Committee to identify and build ski trails, work that was done in collaboration with the White Mountain National Forest and the Civilian Conservation Corps. The committee included three members significant to the development of skiing in the Franconia area: Kate Peckett; Ski Club Hochgebirge founding member Alexander Bright of Boston, who in 1933 also introduced the idea of erecting an aerial tramway in New Hampshire and would be instrumental to seeing such a lift installed at Cannon Mountain in 1938; and Manchester attorney John Carleton.[24]

Carleton's role in developing skiing in Franconia would continue for many years. A Dartmouth graduate, he had competed in the first Winter Olympics in 1924 and made the first documented descent of the headwall of Mount Washington's Tuckerman Ravine several years later.[25] In 1934, he would become the first chairman of the state's Aerial Tramway Commission, and he would continue to lobby for skiing improvements on Cannon into the 1950s. He later served as the treasurer of Mittersill. Carleton was inducted into the U.S. National Ski Hall of Fame in 1968.

Completing the Taft was thus turned over to the CCC, which in the next several years would build dozens of ski trails in New Hampshire. By 1934, New Hampshire listed forty-eight named ski runs, most of which were cut at least in part by the CCC, including the Coppermine and Tucker Brook Trails in Franconia.[26] But the Taft was the first, and it instantly became a draw to skiers and the preferred site of many ski races for decades after its creation.

While the trail was not completed until the summer of 1933, a portion of it was run by many eager skiers during the winter of 1932–33. The honor

A female ski racer careens down the Taft Race Trail before a crowd of onlookers. Charles Trask photo, NESM Collection.

of the first descent, in February 1933, went to Sig Buchmayr, who awed bystanders with a flawless run. The *Ski Bulletin*, a weekly publication out of Boston, reported, "Sigmund Buchmayer [*sic*] lifted the curtain on this new paradise by running the whole course straight, with only a few checks to await his companions, and without a fall."[27]

The first of countless races on the Taft was also held that February, although poor snow cover and protruding tree stumps created something of an obstacle course, causing one ski writer to declare that the trail's most notable first results were "extra patients for the Dartmouth Hospital."[28] In March 1933, the Boston-based Hochgebirge ski club used the Taft to run its annual Hochgebirge Challenge Cup race, held in previous years on the carriage road of Mount Moosilauke. The "Hochies" continued to hold their races on the Taft into the 1950s.

Many ski competitions, both local events and those of regional and national import, were raced on the Taft. Cannon's own Ken Boothroyd was

Mount Lafayette looms across Franconia Notch from this racer on the Taft. *Winston Pote photo, Sugar Hill Historical Museum.*

for a time the record holder for the fastest run, before being unseated by Charley Proctor, then Dick Durrance and finally Toni Matt, who set the lasting pace at two minutes and four seconds.[29]

Competitors, of course, had to hike up the trail before they could race down it. Grooming consisted of skiers sidestepping the trail on their way to the start. Too much snow could be just as problematic as not enough, and sometimes race organizers had to call in extra labor before a competition: "Two days before [a National race on the Taft] was due to be held, we got about two feet of snow," remembered Bunny Nutter, a student during the late 1930s and early '40s at the St. Mary's School for girls in nearby Bethlehem. "We loaded up the truck from St. Mary's…and went over and we sidestepped the whole way up the Taft Racecourse and back down…Boy was that hard work!"[30]

One of the most significant races held on the Taft was the 1946 U.S. Nationals. This was the first National Championship to be held since the eruption of World War II, and the starting list included an impressive roster of notable American skiers—Walter Prager, Toni Matt, Barney McLean, Alexander Bright, Bob Livermore—along with a solid group of local competitors, including Buchmayr, Roger Peabody, Norwood Ball and Bertram Herbert. Paulie Hannah put in a good showing for the Franconia Ski Club in the women's competition, where Austrian emigrant Paula Kann of the Eastern Slope Ski Club won the downhill.[31] Within a few years, Paula would be married to Swiss skier Paul Valar and running the ski school at Cannon Mountain with him.

Although the 1946 event was tinged by tragedy, after twenty-four-year-old army captain Victor Constant was killed during a practice run, when he veered off the trail and hit a tree,[32] it was also something of a homecoming. Many of the racers had only recently returned from serving in World War II, and the race for them was a reunion, with war buddies and old-time local skiers coming together from across the country. "It was really nice meeting all the guys you hadn't seen in a long time," World War II veteran and Franconia native Norwood Ball recalled of the 1946 Nationals. "It was a ball just meeting all the guys…Some of the old guys—Hans Thorner and Sig Buchmayr—participated, and it was really great to sort of get the old gang together again."[33]

The Taft continued to host competitions into the 1950s, but following the 1938 opening of the Cannon Mountain Aerial Tramway, trails were designed to return to the Tram's Valley Station. The race portion of the Taft ended on the opposite side of the mountain, and while a dime would buy a skier a shuttle ride back to the Valley Station, such a journey became too much of a hassle for most skiers. The Taft Racecourse gradually fell to disuse and eventually became overgrown, fading back into the forest from which it was hewn. Despite

Skiers look back at Taft Slalom from the saddle between Cannon and Mount Jackson.
NESM Collection.

its eventual demise, however, the Taft holds an important place in the annals of American ski history, both as the first down-mountain trail created in New England and for the caliber of the early skiers who careened down it. The Taft, that wild and formidable trail, smoothed the way for things to come.

ALEXANDER BRIGHT
AND THE SKI CLUB
HOCHGEBIRGE

In December 1930, some 150 miles south of Cannon Mountain, a group of ten well-heeled Boston bachelors formed the Ski Club Hochgebirge (SCH). Among the founders was Alexander Bright, who would become one of the most influential characters in the development of skiing in Franconia. Bright skied at Peckett's—as well as in Europe—and in 1933 served on New Hampshire's Ski Trails Committee. He was a Harvard alumnus, a prosperous stockbroker from Cambridge and a man who loved competition and going fast—whether on skis, in his LaSalle heading north on Saturday or speeding down a bobsled run in Switzerland.

The founding members of the Ski Club Hochgebirge caught the ski bug early and drove north to spend their winter weekends sliding around carriage roads and hills like the one at Peckett's until the sport developed some heftier terrain. The club did much to encourage ski racing in New Hampshire, establishing an annual race in its first year that continues on the slopes of Cannon each winter. Hochgebirge (which translates from German as "high mountains") members were also involved in creating the National Ski Patrol in the late 1930s and the 10th Mountain Division during World War II, and the club boasts several members in the United States National Ski Hall of Fame. Although the "Hochies" have skied trails and areas throughout the region and beyond, the club's closest and longest ties are to Cannon Mountain, the Ski Club Hochgebirge's "spiritual home and Mother Church."[34]

When that group of ski-crazed bachelors founded the club, skiing was still unknown to most Americans. Lift-served ski areas were years in the future, and anything resembling the ski trails we know today was unheard of. So it took a certain kind of person to spend weekends driving from the city to the hills of New Hampshire and then climbing up narrow carriage roads for one or two ski runs:

> *The enthusiasm of this group developed to the point where they were regarded by their friends and acquaintances as suffering from an intense and peculiar obsession. In all ways they were different from their fellow men…They developed a healthy tan in the midst of winter; and they spoke distastefully of the usually welcome advent of spring.*[35]

The club organized its first race—the Hochgebirge Challenge Cup—in March 1931 on the carriage road of Mount Moosilauke. The inaugural race was a team downhill, and the Hochies finished last out of six teams. But they soon improved their racing skills, and when the competition was moved to the Taft in 1933, the Hochgebirge team schussed into first place. For much of the next decade, the Hochgebirge club was competitive with all the top teams, including the formidable Dartmouth Outing Club.

Since 1933, the Hochgebirge club has held its annual Challenge Cup at Cannon Mountain, missing only a handful of races due to weather and

The 1935 United States FIS team, seen here in Murren, Switzerland, included five SCH members. *From left:* James Lowell (SCH), Alexander Bright (SCH), George Page, G.R. Fearing (SCH), Thomas Dabney (SCH) and Samuel Wakeman (SCH). *Courtesy Ski Club Hochgebirge.*

during World War II. The Hochies teamed up with the Franconia Ski Club in 1946 to host the first postwar U.S. Nationals in conjunction with the Challenge Cup, and in 1955, the Hochgebirge race was used as the Olympic team tryouts.[36] The race has evolved from a combined downhill and slalom including the country's top male ski racers to a New England Masters Series slalom for racers aged eighteen to eighty-plus. Women were first invited to compete in the Hochgebirge race in 1974, although they were not admitted to the Hochgebirge club as members until 1988.[37]

Competition was not limited to the annual Challenge Cup. The early Hochies were always ready for a challenge and an adventure, as demonstrated by their staging of the thrilling American Inferno race on Mount Washington in April 1933. The race ran from the summit of Mount Washington over the dauntingly steep headwall of Tuckerman Ravine and into Pinkham Notch, with skiers dropping some forty-three hundred vertical feet. The winning time the first year was nearly fifteen minutes, an eternity compared with modern races that last at most a few minutes.[38] The full-length Inferno was held only three times—in 1933, 1934 and 1939. It was during the last full Inferno that the recently immigrated Austrian Toni Matt made his legendary straight run of the ravine, completing the summit-to-base race in just under six minutes and thrilling spectators en route to his win.[39]

In the first American Inferno, Bright claimed second place, with fellow Hochies John Lawrence, Sam Wakeman and John Sherburne finishing third, fourth and eighth.[40] Sherburne, a founding member of the club, was "an enthusiastic skier who loved Mt. Washington's Ravine…a delightful man in every way—friendly, gregarious, cheerful, intelligent, gentlemanly."[41] He died a young man, not long after the 1934 Inferno, and the Sherburne Trail on Mount Washington, running from Tuckerman Ravine to Pinkham Notch, is named for him. (Two weather-shortened versions of the race were held in 1952 [Bobtail Inferno] and 1969 [Inferno Giant Slalom]. Duncan Cullman, who grew up skiing on Cannon's slopes and was briefly a member of the U.S. Ski Team, eked out a victory in the 1969 race.)[42]

Club members also enjoyed the revelry that was an integral part of skiing in its early days. It was common to follow a day of climbing and skiing with an evening of singing and drinking, then to get up early the next morning to ski some more. After Bright's death in 1980, his son, Cameron, found among his father's possessions about fifteen hundred Hochgebirge song pamphlets. In the club's earliest days, SCH members stayed in various ski lodges, many of them in and around Franconia. In 1959, the club bought a house on Coal

Hill Road in Franconia,[43] which was soon dubbed the "Hochie Hilton" and which remains club headquarters.

By this time, the club had evolved from its original core of skiing bachelors into a family affair, and the house was often crowded with a mix of merry adults and boisterous youngsters. "There were always a ton of kids. We'd just be basically racing around, playing…hide-and-go-seek or jumping down the laundry chute," said Cameron Bright. "I have absolutely no memory of what any adult did. I just remember it was always this huge kid tornado."[44] In 2011, the Ski Club Hochgebirge included about 125 members, with some families counting several generations in the club. The spirit of racing and the fellowship of skiing remain strong among the Hochies. Sometimes they even break into song by the fire after a day of skiing.

Hochgebirgers have had considerable influence on the evolution of American skiing. Bright and Bob Livermore were both on the United States ski team for the 1936 Olympics in Germany, the first Olympic Games to include alpine skiing events. Following the Olympics, they were involved in forming the National Ski Patrol (NSP) and the legendary 10th Mountain Division, in which Livermore served during World War II. (Bright served in the Air Corps during the war and was stationed in England.)[45] Bright and

SCH racing star Carolyn Beckedorff cruises to victory in the 2010 Hochgebirge Challenge Cup at Cannon. *Photo courtesy Paul Hayes/Record-Littleton.*

Livermore were among the first to pass the NSP test in the late 1930s. While Bright never worked as a ski patroller—although he certainly incurred plenty of ski injuries—Livermore was very involved in developing the ski patrol in the East and was the first chairman of the Eastern Division of the NSP.[46]

Several other Hochies have skied in the Olympics—George Macomber, Ralph Miller, Brooks Dodge and honorary member Clarita Heath Bright among them. Bright and Livermore are both members of the U.S. National Ski Hall of Fame, along with Hochies Malcolm McLane and George Macomber, who were founders of the Wildcat Mountain Ski Area in the 1950s and made countless contributions to American skiing.

It was Bright, however, who played the most direct role in the development of Cannon Mountain. From the start, he was part of the skiing landscape around Franconia and was widely known in skiing circles. Part of his skiing reputation was as a member of the "broken bones club," and there was a turn on the Taft Race Trail known as "Bright's Corner" after he careened off course during a race in the 1930s, landing in the woods with three broken ribs.[47] The Bostonian was also known for reasons beyond his skiing prowess. "Alec…was very famous in New Hampshire because every state trooper… had stopped him on his way to go skiing," recalled Roger Peabody.[48]

When skiing needed an advocate, Bright stepped up again and again—helping to convince the state to build a tramway at Cannon in the 1930s and returning to the state legislature in the early 1950s to lobby for much-needed skiing improvements at the mountain. He played a key role in bringing an aerial tramway, the first at a ski area in North America, to Cannon. When it opened in 1938—some five years after Bright first introduced the idea—the Cannon Mountain Aerial Tramway earned Cannon and Franconia a secure place at the apex of the American ski scene.

Bright had skied in Switzerland in 1930 and had seen Europe's aerial tramways and the benefits they offered to ski centers. While New England skiers were spending hours toiling uphill for one or two downhill runs a day, skiers in Europe were whisked to mountain summits in mere minutes, allowing them to enjoy the thrill of the descent more often on less tired legs. In December 1933, at a meeting of the New England Council devoted to generating ideas for promotion and development of skiing in the region, Bright proposed developing aerial tramways in New England for use by both skiers and warm-weather visitors. For the next several years, he worked tirelessly to make the tramway dream a reality, serving on the state Tramway Commission established in 1934 to study the issue,[49] helping to conduct a survey of twenty New Hampshire mountains as potential locations that summer and continuing to lobby for a tramway until the state legislature approved the concept, funded it and eventually constructed the Cannon tramway.

"He had a passion for skiing, and…he had seen in Europe that they had a tramway, and he thought, 'This is the future of skiing, and if we're going to have skiing in New England, we need to move along. We can't just all ski at Peckett's in Sugar Hill,'" said Cameron Bright of his father. "To him, I think that was a glorious time…But I think he felt that if [skiing] was going to be a big sport with lots of people doing it…that you needed to do it in the best way."[50]

Alec Bright's devotion to the sport and his prowess on the hill endeared him to his skiing companions. When American skiing began to take off, many skiers were young college men or recent graduates. Bright, born in 1897, was a decade or more older than most skiers of the time and earned the affectionate nickname "Grandpa Bright." He came to other things later in life, too, including marriage. He married his (much younger) 1936 Olympic teammate Clarita Heath at the age of sixty-two and became a father soon after. His extra years didn't slow him down much, as evidenced by a slew of top-ten finishes in races from the Challenge Cup on Cannon to the Inferno on Washington. His racing record fills an entire page of the Hochgebirge's

Alec Bright races on the Taft in 1938. *Charles Trask photo, NESM Collection.*

1938 history and includes races from Sun Valley, California, to Murren, Switzerland. Among Bright's top finishes was a first place in the Eastern Downhill Championship and Olympic Tryouts held on Mount Washington in 1935, with which he earned his berth on the 1936 Olympic Ski Team.[51] Grandpa Bright was thirty-eight years old at those Games.

Bright continued ski racing through middle age and into senior citizenship. He competed in the Hochgebirge Challenge Cup on Cannon well into his seventies, retaining the old-fashioned stem turns from his early days of skiing. Throughout his life, whether he was skiing in New Hampshire or the European Alps, Bright remained true to his New England roots.

"I think he was just very proud of New England skiing in general… The mountains were small, and they were skiing maybe not in the perfect conditions and other things, but the skiing was really good. And the skiers were really good," said Cameron Bright. "He said to me that I should always remember how incredibly lucky I was to grow up skiing at Cannon Mountain, because if you could ski on Cannon Mountain, you could really ski comfortably anywhere else in the world."[52]

CANNON MOUNTAIN AERIAL TRAMWAY

Reaching New Heights

A series of serendipitous events through the 1930s contributed to Franconia's rise as a ski center: the ski school at Peckett's, construction of the Taft Trail, and the Hochgebirgers and their introduction of racing to the local ski scene. But it was the 1938 opening of the first passenger aerial tramway in North America that cemented Cannon's place at the summit of American skiing and launched the mountain's development as a modern ski area.

The idea of building an aerial tramway in New Hampshire was introduced in 1933 by Alec Bright and was intriguing enough to garner national attention. At the time, there were no means of uphill travel at ski slopes in the United States. The first rope tow would open in January 1934 in Woodstock, Vermont; the J-bar lift would not be introduced for two more years; and the chairlift, which became the favorite of ski areas everywhere, would not make its world debut until 1936 in Sun Valley, and not in the East until 1937, at the Belknap Recreation Area in New Hampshire.[53] The thrill of a mountain descent in the early 1930s came only after a strenuous climb.

Aerial tramways were newly popular at European ski areas and had long been used in the western United States for mining operations.[54] An early version of the gondola (sometimes referred to as a "tramway") had even carried sightseers to Sunrise Peak in Silver Plume, Colorado, from 1907 until 1914.[55] But passenger lifts at ski areas were a novel concept when Bright, speaking for the Ski Club Hochgebirge, presented the tramway idea during a December 1933 meeting of the New England Council.

The tram ascends Cannon, with Mount Lafayette in the background. The original tramcars had headlights for nighttime travel and ski racks, both visible in this photo. *NESM Collection.*

"Aerial cableways…may be the next and most spectacular manifestation of the ski craze which is sweeping over New England," read a report of that meeting in the *Boston Evening Transcript.* The article, as did many subsequent reports appearing in newspapers throughout New England and beyond, noted the popularity and success of tramways in Europe and hypothesized that aerial tramways could turn New England into the "Switzerland of America."[56]

Bright made several arguments in support of building a tramway in New Hampshire: greater access to the sport for novice skiers, more time devoted to skiing downhill than to trudging uphill, reduced congestion on slopes carrying both upward- and downward-bound skiers, and enabling New England to lay claim as a major ski center.[57] "With a tramway the slopes of Cannon will be alive with skiers," Bright wrote in 1934. "An aerial tramway completed on Cannon Mountain—the first in the United States…would quickly herald from California to Florida in convincing terms the certainty and availability [of] winter sports [and] the guaranteed snow conditions in New England's mountains."[58]

In the midst of the Great Depression, it was critical that the tramway be portrayed as a profitable venture for the state. So while it was skiers who introduced the concept, it was the potential appeal to warmer-weather vista seekers—the numerous visitors to Franconia Notch each summer and fall—that sold the aerial tramway concept. In May 1934, New Hampshire governor John Winant appointed a commission to study the feasibility of erecting an aerial tramway in the state. Manchester attorney John Carleton was named chairman of the committee, which also included Alec Bright.

During the summer of 1934, the commission collaborated with the Worcester, Massachusetts–based American Steel & Wire Company to survey twenty-one potential tramway sites. American Steel & Wire, the American representative of European tramway company Bleichert-Zuegg, was a "pioneer in tramway construction," operating hundreds of freight trams in North and South America.[59] Beginning in the late 1930s, American Steel & Wire would also build many of the earliest chairlifts at American ski areas.[60]

The survey of New Hampshire mountains included such varied peaks as solitary Mount Manadnock in the south and lofty Mount Washington to the north. It included four potential locations in Franconia Notch: Cannon, Mount Liberty and two routes on Mount Lafayette. Cannon and Mount Moosilauke, just southwest of Franconia Notch, emerged as early and clear favorites and were presented as such when Carleton's committee reported to the state in August 1934.

Both mountains offered good snow cover. Moosilauke, long a favorite of Dartmouth Outing Club (DOC) skiers, offered a vertical descent of 2,470 feet. Cannon's descent of 1,320 feet was considerably shorter, but it was along a well-traveled route. While some sixteen hundred people passed along the Lost River Road access point to Moosilauke throughout the summer and fall, an estimated two million visitors traveled through Franconia Notch each year. Cannon was also close to the highway and to a source of electric power, and the proposed location would be obscured from the scenic road through the Notch.[61]

Bright, who authored the 1934 survey report, clearly favored building the tramway on Cannon Mountain. In September, when some members of the Dartmouth Outing Club opposed the idea of building a tramway on Mount Moosilauke, the DOC removed its support for the venture on its home mountain, and Cannon was left as the sole contender for the project.

Among the earliest proponents for a Cannon Tramway was Roland Peabody, who had undoubtedly run into Bright at Peckett's and other local skiing haunts. Born and raised in Franconia, Peabody was a skier and the proprietor of the local grocery and hardware store. His knowledge of the area and his support of Bright's idea were crucial in seeing the Cannon Mountain Aerial Tramway project to fruition. Peabody helped nudge the idea through the state legislature and became the first manager of the tramway.

In 1935, the New Hampshire state legislature approved a bill to create a five-member Tramway Commission to construct and operate an aerial tramway. The commission, again headed by Carleton, was authorized to accept federal grants—with its sights set on Public Works Administration funds—and other means of financing the $200,000 project. Federal funding didn't materialize, however, and the tramway venture was put on hold. Bright, Peabody and other supporters persevered, and in June 1937, the legislature passed a new bill authorizing $250,000 in state funding to build the Cannon Mountain Aerial Tramway.[62]

Former state executive councilor James MacLeod of Littleton was appointed chairman of a new Tramway Commission. It hired Roland Peabody as the first managing director of the tramway, a role he would

Workers labor 115 feet above the ground to assemble parts of the top tower of the tramway in 1938. *Cannon Mountain files.*

maintain until his death in 1950, ably leading Cannon through its first years as a ski area. Peabody set up an office in the Iron Mine Tavern in Franconia, and the work to build the tramway began nearly immediately, continuing through the winter, when snow squalls, gusty winds and icy temperatures are the norm in Franconia Notch. As work progressed, the tramway project was noted as a marvel in both engineering and skiing in newspapers around New Hampshire, in Boston and New York and in publications as far afield as Oregon and Illinois.

The project included altering the route of the highway through the Notch, constructing parking areas and a highway underpass for skiers to access the Valley Station and building new ski trails. In August, a day after winning the contract for erecting the tramway with a bid of $191,974.99,[63] American Steel & Wire began survey work on the proposed tramway line. Clearing for the Valley Station—to be located near the site of the former Profile House—was complete by the end of August, as was the relocation of the highway and authorization to bring a crew of some two hundred Civilian Conservation Corps men to nearby North Woodstock to build a parking area, construct an observation platform at Cannon's summit and cut new foot and ski trails.[64]

Teams of men carried cement, cable and other materials up the mountain, traversing dense undergrowth, mud and huge boulders to construct a freight tram. This tram hauled workers, supplies and steel to construct the tramway's three towers. During the winter, the construction crew poured thirty-two carloads of cement and assembled 232 tons of steel and four miles of cable by hand.[65] In March 1938, two reels of steel cable, each weighing some 30 tons, were shipped via train from Trenton, New Jersey, to Lincoln, New Hampshire, and transported through the Notch by truck to the base of the tramway site. The steel for the three tramway towers arrived by the same route.[66]

Throughout the spring, the towers—standing 115 feet, 94 feet and 88 feet tall—were erected and painted to blend in with the scenery, the 5,410 feet of cable was run, and the Valley and Mountain stations were completed.[67] The Cannon Mountain Aerial Tramway, five years after the discussion began and nine months after ground was broken on the project, was slated to open in May, but inclement mountain weather delayed the opening date twice, moving it ultimately to June 28, 1938.

Some one hundred newspaper and newsreel reporters and photographers had been treated to a preview of the tramway on June 20, complete with a tour of the summit by Roland Peabody's mountain guides. The guides wore "natty blue uniforms and hats" and pointed out the myriad peaks visible from the top of Cannon, where the view on a clear day stretches into Vermont, Maine and Canada. Photographers "climbed all over the place," reported the *Littleton Courier* on June 23, trying to get the best angle to showcase "just what New Hampshire has in the way of a new thrill."[68] Miss New Hampshire 1938, Lorraine Ledoux of Littleton, was photographed leaning from a tramcar window and waving to the camera.

At a time when few Americans had been suspended in the air in any form— airplane, chairlift, hot-air balloon—the tramway must have seemed thrilling indeed. Many of its first passengers had probably never been to the top of a mountain, and so it was not only the ride that was fascinating but also the bird's-eye view from the summit. "The sensation of passing up over the rough forest terrain of the mountainside could be had in nothing short of an airplane ride," wrote one reporter. "The panorama was spread out, a sight before available only to those individuals hardy enough to climb on foot to the top of Cannon."[69]

With the hubbub surrounding the Cannon Tramway, it was hardly surprising that a crowd of more than 700 flocked to the opening. Some 350 of those were invited guests—state officials, governors from other New England states, Tramway Commission members and representatives from American Steel & Wire. New Hampshire's first lady, with water from Echo Lake at the base of Cannon Mountain, christened the tramcars—named Lafayette and Lincoln after nearby peaks. Governor Francis Murphy lauded the accomplishment of opening the country's first aerial passenger tramway:

> *It is a spectacular but perfectly practical public venture which…has had measurable good effect upon the public spirit…In a little more than five minutes time on the tramway you will have made an ascent which it takes a trained athlete an hour and a half to make over the trail afoot. The tramway has thus removed the handicaps of age and health, and has made the mountain top accessible to all.[70]*

The Cannon Mountain Aerial Tramway was an instant success. More than 100,000 people rode the tram in its first summer of operation, with another 37,000 climbing onboard during the winter of 1938–39.[71] Within a week of its opening, the tram carried its first wedding party, Hilda Blodgett of Littleton and Arthur Blaney of Bethlehem, who wed at Cannon's summit during a July 4 weekend that saw some 2,600 others enjoy the tram, despite poor weather.[72] Popular radio commentator and ski enthusiast Lowell Thomas was among the tramway's visitors that first winter, making a live broadcast from the Mountain Station in January 1939.

In the early years, the tram was the only lift to the top of Cannon, and long lines at the Valley Station were a common occurrence. *Charles Trask photo.*

The tram rose 2,022 vertical feet from Valley Station to Mountain Station. Each twelve-sided tramcar was suspended by a wheeled carriage from a single traction cable. As one car left the Valley Station, the other would begin its descent from the Mountain Station, pulled by another cable operated by a one-hundred-horse-power engine. Early brochures for the tram made note of the lift's safety and the hand and foot controls used by the operator at the Valley Station to slow, stop and accelerate the cars. The conductor inside each tramcar communicated with the operator through push buttons and telephone. Edgar Herbert was among the first operators, and "he could tell just [by] the vibration if there was anything going on up there. He'd stop that thing before the guys could push the button."[73]

Each morning, an aerial lift mechanic would ride on top of the first tramcar up the mountain, stopping at each tower to chip ice off the cable wheels.[74] (Lift mechanics still take this early morning ride, but the tramcars are considerably larger.) On windy days, "lunch box" weights were distributed around the inside of each tramcar to decrease sway, and the operator would slow the cars as they approached the towers so the conductors in each car

A crew of shovelers clears a path through deep snow, allowing tramcars access to the Mountain Station. *Charles Trask photo, NESM Collection.*

could open the doors and push off the towers with their feet.[75] The original tramcars also hung lower to the ground approaching the Mountain Station than today's tramway. After a big snowstorm, crews of men would ride the tram as far up the mountain as the snowdrifts allowed and then jump out and shovel a path for the tramcar to continue its ascent.[76]

Skiers finding their way up the tram during its first winter of operation had few options for descending. Taft Slalom would carry them to the Taft Racecourse, Coppermine and Tucker Brook Trails over the saddle, ending a considerable distance from the tram's Valley Station. Or they could ride the sweeping corners of the new Cannon Mountain Trail and cut back to the base of the tram. A single ride to the top cost sixty cents, and skiers could purchase ten rides for five dollars.[77]

Aerial tramways were considered one of the safest forms of transportation when the Cannon Tramway began operation, and in its seventy-plus years, there has been only one major mishap. On March 12, 1963, twenty-year-old tram operator Ronald Broderick of Franconia was returning to the

Valley Station in the Lincoln car after transporting ski patrollers and other mountain staff to the summit on a routine early morning run when a rogue gust of wind lifted the car off the tram cable. The car plunged ninety feet to the ground. It took nearly two hours for rescuers to navigate the boulder-strewn tramline and carry Broderick to the Valley Station. He suffered a fractured skull, a broken arm and a broken leg.[78] The ensuing investigation revealed that a "cyclonic blast of wind" was to blame for the fluke accident,[79] and while the tram remained closed until summer, it resumed operation and continued without further incident until its retirement in 1980, when Tram II was installed. Broderick recovered and continued to work at the mountain for decades after his frightening fall.

The fallen tramcar was deemed beyond repair, and the state retained Colorado-based Heron Engineering Company to build a new tramcar.[80] During the 1960s, the tramcars were painted red and white. One of the three original tramcars is in storage at Cannon Mountain. The other two rest within miles of the Valley Station: one at the entrance of the New

Workers survey the damage to the tramcar that fell some ninety feet from the cable to the ground in 1963. *Cannon Mountain files.*

This 1980 photo is a juxtaposition of old and new, with the original tramcar and Mountain Station (at left) dwarfed by the new. *Gary Harwood photo.*

England Ski Museum near the base of the tramway, the other at local tourist attraction Clark's Trading Post in Lincoln.

By the 1970s, it was clear that what was once a sensation in the skiing world had become antiquated, and in 1978, work began on the construction of a new aerial tramway at Cannon Mountain. Tram II, dedicated in May 1980, is faster—four minutes, forty-two seconds from valley to summit—and bigger, with an eighty-person capacity for each tramcar. Its hourly passenger volume, at 1,540 (770 each direction), is three times the original tram, and its shiny red and yellow cars—nicknamed Ketchup and Mustard—are brighter and more modern.

Construction of the new tramway did not require such a massive amount of manpower as had the original. The old tram was used to transport materials, and helicopters airlifted the bulkiest pieces required for construction. The Italian company Nuova Agudio installed Tram II at a cost of $4.6 million.[81] On May 24, 1980, a crowd of nearly five thousand attended the dedication of the new tramway. This included eight hundred invited guests, among them Damus Champagne, one of Cannon's earliest aerial tramway mechanics, and former New Hampshire governors Sherman Adams and Hugh Gregg.[82]

The tram descends past the backdrop of Mount Lafayette and frosted trees after leaving skiers at the summit in 2011. *Author photo*.

The original Cannon Mountain Aerial Tramway carried 6,581,338 passengers in its forty-two years.[83] Tram II carried roughly the same number in its first three decades. More than seventy-five years after Alec Bright made his tramway proposal, the Cannon Mountain Aerial Tramway remains a popular man-made complement to the natural wonders that have drawn visitors to Franconia Notch for more than two centuries. And while the novelty of such a lift has faded with time and experience, a ride up the tram in any season remains a thrill of dizzying heights and magnificent vistas.

ROLAND PEABODY

The Father of Cannon Mountain

Roland Peabody was an innovator in American ski area development. He had to be. There was no model to follow when he became manager of the Cannon Mountain Aerial Tramway; no design for ski lodges, no blueprint for adding ski lifts and trails to a mountain, no snowmaking or grooming equipment. There was just a mountain owned by the State of New Hampshire, a growing number of New Englanders becoming passionate about skiing and an unimaginable amount of work to do to build a thriving ski center. With the opening of the tram in 1938, Peabody established a summer guide service at the summit of Cannon and the country's first professional ski patrol, developed races for skiers of varying abilities at the mountain and introduced countless young skiers to the sport.

A diligent worker, insightful businessman and quintessential diplomat, Peabody's "sincere and friendly manner endeared him not only to those who worked for him, but to the great throngs of skiers and other visitors to the tramway and business associates and neighbors throughout the North Country with whom he came in contact."[84] He was a champion of his hometown of Franconia, serving the town in a number of official roles throughout his life. But it was Cannon Mountain, which continues to contribute to the economy and spirit of the town, that became his most lasting legacy. From the waning years of the Great Depression to the postwar boom, Peabody nurtured the mountain from a fledgling ski area with a single lift and a smattering of ski trails into a leader in the emerging ski industry.

Roland Peabody skis the Cannon Trail, circa 1940. *Charles Trask photo, NESM Collection.*

Peabody was born in Franconia in 1900 and lived his life in the village. He enlisted in the army in 1918, spent a year serving in France during World War I and was honorably discharged with the rank of corporal. He returned to Franconia, married Nina Whipple and went to work for his father's construction business, H.A. Peabody & Son, which employed some two hundred men at its height and built many of the area's earliest vacation homes. Peabody later ran a general store in town. From 1920 through 1948, he served in various elected town positions, including selectman, school district treasurer and town moderator. He also worked as a wintertime guide at Peckett's-on-Sugar Hill before Kate Peckett organized the ski school there, leading guests on snowy outings wearing snowshoes or touring skis. When the ski school was established at Peckett's, Roland Peabody was among its first students and was soon proficient enough to open his own Franconia Ski School, which he ran from his store.[85]

In 1935, before there was any certification process for professional instructors, Peabody was awarded the U.S. Eastern Amateur Ski Association's

Certificate No. 1 as a qualified "Amateur Ski Instructor."[86] A few years later, he collaborated with other leaders in American skiing to develop the first professional ski instructor certification system. For many years, Cannon hosted ski instructors' testing, with Peabody acting as the head examiner, assisted by such skiing stars as Walter Prager and Benno Rybizka.[87]

In 1933, with Robert "Father" Peckett and other area business leaders and ski enthusiasts, Peabody founded the Franconia Ski Club, which remains active today as a junior race training program. In its earliest years, the club endeavored to provide social and recreational opportunities for area residents of all ages and to expand the prospects of skiing—through promotion of the area, ski instruction and trail development—for both locals and visitors. The reasoning was that attracting skiers to the area would boost the local economy, providing wintertime business for lodging and dining establishments. Peabody was the first president of the Franconia Ski Club and headed the organization until 1937, when he went to work for the state as manager of the Cannon Mountain Aerial Tramway.

Peabody and other leaders of the local ski movement in the 1930s understood that forming a club and cutting a few trails would not be enough to corner the skiing market. He was one of the first to support Alec Bright's proposal to build a tramway at Cannon. Believing such a lift would expand winter business in the region, Peabody set to work persuading the legislature to approve and fund the construction of a tramway. When the state finally came through in 1937, Roland Peabody was the obvious choice to oversee the tramway: he had his finger on the pulse of skiing and of Franconia.

He was adept both at managing the tramway's team of employees and welcoming the innumerable visitors to the Notch in all seasons. Perhaps more importantly, Peabody understood the intricacies of working with the Tramway Commission and the bulky state legislature (with twenty-four senators and four hundred representatives, New Hampshire's General Court is among the largest legislative bodies in the world),[88] whose members did not all comprehend or particularly care about skiing and its growing importance to the local economy. "Roland was quite the politician. He made a good one to represent the Tramway with the state," said Ray Martin, who came to Franconia in 1940 to work at Peckett's and was later a trustee of the Roland Peabody Memorial Fund. "He had to answer to all these commissioners and so on."[89]

When the tramway opened in the summer of 1938, it was the first time visitors in large numbers had been set loose to wander around the summit, generally wearing regular street clothes and shoes. Each tramcar was greeted

Famous radio and television commentator Lowell Thomas (center) broadcasts from the tramway in the late 1930s. Roland Peabody is at left. *Charles Trask photo, NESM Collection.*

by a neatly dressed mountain guide, who would lead passengers along the Rim Trail at the summit, pointing out various peaks in the panoramic vista and answering questions. The guide service became the victim of budget cuts some years later, but it was an important part of the tramway's early success.

Many of the guides swapped their summer uniforms for ski patrol parkas during the winter. With the tramway exponentially increasing the numbers of skiers using Cannon's trails, Peabody knew the snow cover would deteriorate relatively quickly. In the winter of 1938–39, he established the country's first professional ski patrol on Cannon, which acted as both trail maintenance crew and first aid providers.[90]

One member of the original Cannon Mountain ski patrol members was Sel Hannah, who had a hand in much of the mountain's early trail development. He called Peabody "a man of vision…[who] foresaw that ski racing could be a great factor in making Franconia known as a ski center."[91] Hannah succeeded Peabody as president of the Franconia Ski Club, and the pair worked together for many years to develop racing at Cannon.

Beyond his continued support of the ski club's activities at Cannon, Peabody established the weekly "time trials" on the Cannon Mountain Trail. (The trail is now split into Upper, Middle and Lower Cannon and is wider and straighter than when it was first built as one long, winding run.) Each Wednesday, skiers would attempt to run the trail, from mountain summit to base, in less than three and a half minutes to earn a Gold Cannon pin. Silver Cannons were awarded to those with slightly higher times, and Bronze Cannons were given to racers who finished close to the time they predicted it would take them to complete the run.

The Gold Cannon was coveted by ski racers, and some competitors were known to pack out lines tight to the corners or through the woods in an effort to shorten their times. Roger Peabody, Roland's son, earned several Gold Cannons and held the course record for many years. The last Cannon races were in 1962, when former Franconia Ski Club kids and then U.S. Ski Team members Gordi Eaton and Joan Hannah (Sel's daughter) retired the records.[92]

In 1942, at a time when ski racing had strict classifications and competition was often fierce, Peabody also introduced racing events for recreational skiers looking "to try their skill in competition without fear of being hopelessly outclassed," thus giving "the so-called recreational skier something more to shoot at than a day of hit or miss floundering around on his own."[93] The races proved popular, with some fifty men and women entered in the first competition, which included both slalom and downhill runs.[94]

Largely through Roland Peabody's efforts, Cannon's popularity grew throughout World War II and in the immediate postwar years. By all accounts, Peabody was ardently devoted to his job as the top gun at Cannon Mountain, arriving first thing each morning, seven days a week. In the end, that may have been his undoing. Roland Peabody died on January 31, 1950, at the young age of fifty, after suffering a heart attack.

Roger Peabody was quickly appointed managing director of the Cannon Mountain Aerial Tramway after his father's death. He had worked at Cannon since the tram opened, beginning as a guide and holding a variety of positions up to 1950. For a couple of years, Roger also acted as night watchman, and he and his wife, Louise, lived at the Summit Station of the tramway, with their first child, Jere, who was then an infant. "My dad used to ski up and down with me in a wicker basket on his back," Jere Peabody recalled. "People used to come in and remind me that I used to hide my teddy bears behind the radiators [at the tram station]."[95] Roger was manager at Cannon until moving on to become the first paid executive director of

Roland Peabody. *NESM Collection.*

the U.S. Eastern Amateur Ski Association in 1954, where he continued to influence skiing in the region.

After Roger, several of his six children worked on the mountain. Jere and Joel Peabody were members of the Cannon Mountain ski patrol for many years, with Joel retiring in 2003 after more than thirty years at the mountain. Brother Jon Peabody ran the Old Man concessions in the Notch for some time, and sister Jennifer Peabody Gaudette worked as an administrator at the mountain from the late 1970s though the late '80s. "The mountain to me was always family," said Joel in 2008. "I built my house so I could look out the window at it all day long."[96] The third generation of Peabodys has retired from the mountain now, but Roland Peabody's great-grandson, Tyler Gaudette, who grew up speeding along the slopes his great-grandfather and grandfather helped cultivate so long ago, began work on the ski patrol during the winter of 2010–11.

The Peabody name is stamped all over the mountain. In the mid-1950s, the state approved an expansion at Cannon, naming the new area the Roland Peabody Memorial Slopes. There remains a Peabody Base Lodge and a Peabody chairlift, and the light atop Cannon once dubbed "Peabody's Planet"[97] still acts as a beacon for those who gaze at the nighttime mountain from afar.

A few years after Roland Peabody died, the Franconia Ski Club established a Roland Peabody Memorial Fund dedicated to introducing local children to the sport. Over the next few decades, the fund provided inexpensive rentals of skis, boots and poles to hundreds of young skiers. The club also dedicated its annual interscholastic meet the Roland Peabody Memorial Race. In the 1980s, after several years of declining interest in renting equipment, the fund discontinued that aspect of the program. But the annual race continues. More than a half century after Peabody's death, children from Franconia and Sugar Hill, Lincoln and Woodstock, Littleton and Bethlehem and occasionally other nearby towns converge on Cannon Mountain one day each February to ski and compete in his name. The race is a team competition for third through sixth graders, and for many of the young skiers it is an introduction to ski racing.

"The kids just love it. They have a great day," said Jennifer Gaudette, who never knew her grandfather but has helped orchestrate the Roland Peabody Memorial Race for more than three decades and is the treasurer of the fund. "For us it's just the joy of that third grader who's never [raced]. It's just so much fun to watch."[98]

Each year, the school name of the winning team is engraved on a plaque below the bronze likeness of Roland Peabody, which hangs in the tram's Valley Station. Thousands of skiers file by Peabody's image each winter on their way to board the tram. And so, in a way, the man who did so much to provide skiing opportunities for area youngsters and to establish Cannon as a major ski center continues to watch over the mountain and its skiers.

CANNON MOUNTAIN SKI PATROL

First Professional Patrol in the United States

When the tramway opened in June 1938, Roland Peabody hired about a dozen men to work as guides during the summer and as ski patrollers for the winter. The National Ski Patrol was just being organized, and a volunteer patrol had been established at Mount Mansfield in Vermont a few years earlier, but Cannon's was the first paid ski patrol outfit in the country. Peabody supported the development of the NSP and was adamant that his patrollers become members.[99] By today's standards, the early ski patrol efforts were primitive—the most basic medical training, heavy and unwieldy toboggans and communication via phone boxes scattered around the mountain.

Cannon's earliest patrollers were charged not only with responding to skiers in need of assistance but also with maintaining ski slopes to keep them safe. They created equipment for transporting skiers and for grooming trails, helped develop training guidelines in an emerging field and set a professional standard that is maintained by the Cannon Mountain Ski Patrol today. "The original guys were unbelievable. They were the first, and they were good," said Jere Peabody, who joined the ski patrol as a teenager in the late 1950s. "It was really a great thing to work on [patrol] and be involved in that."[100]

The role of ski patrollers has evolved over the years. Virtually all the equipment used for the job has changed from the early days. Toboggans are lighter and more maneuverable, radios allow instant communication between patrollers, and everything from skis to medical equipment is considerably more high tech. Cannon's patrol roster now contains some forty names,

The original Cannon Mountain Ski Patrol, 1938. *From left*: Don Fulton, Joe Chapman, Sel Hannah, Archie Herbert, James Cyr, Herb Brooks and head of patrol Ken Boothroyd. *NESM Collection*.

including about a dozen full-time patrollers, a weekend crew of eight and a slew of patrol volunteers. Medical training ranges from Outdoor Emergency Care certification to full paramedic. Patrollers are no longer charged with grooming ski trails, but they are responsible for keeping the mountain as safe as possible and for providing first-rate medical care in a difficult location.

First aid training for the earliest patrollers at Cannon was minimal. "We were all more or less amateurs in first aid," recalled Ken Boothroyd, who headed the first Cannon Mountain ski patrol. "I had taken a standard first aid course, but that's all the training I had at the time, and we sort of improvised a lot in the beginning."[101] The main misery of injured skiers often came from being stranded in the snow, waiting for help to arrive. In the days before constant radio communication, it sometimes took half an hour or longer for patrollers to arrive at the scene of an accident. Often, the aid offered by patrollers was simply to keep the injured skiers warm and transport them down the mountain.

By the tramway's second winter, all Cannon ski patrollers were "first-aid qualified" through the completion of a twenty-four-hour course with the American Red Cross. The patrol also worked with local doctors, who provided some medical training before there was such a thing as an emergency medical technician. Physicians Frank Dudley, Harry McDade, Jim Bogle and Charles Copenhaver were not only medical professionals but also "skiing nuts" and added depth to the early Cannon patrol.[102]

With no model to follow, the early patrollers improvised equipment for doing their work. Emergency toboggans, used to transport injured skiers down the mountain, were crafted using regular wooden sledding toboggans. These were reinforced with steel rails along the sides and two ropes tied to the front and back. One patroller would straddle the front end of the toboggan holding the front rope, with another patroller at the back rope acting as brakeman.[103] During World War II, with Cannon's staff cut to a skeleton crew of eight employees and the paid patrol replaced by volunteers, Roger Peabody and local Swiss instructor Hans Thorner rigged up a lighter-weight toboggan with long handles that could be managed by one man if necessary.[104] Eventually, the brake system evolved to a steel bear-claw contraption attached to the back of

A ski patroller stands ready with a toboggan, circa 1960s. *Courtesy Bill Mead.*

the toboggan, which would dig into the snow to help patrollers control the sled.[105]

Like today's ski patrol, Cannon's original crew was responsible for ensuring the safety of people traveling both up and down the mountain. In the fall of the second year of the tram's operation, the ski patrol had to evacuate both tramcars when they became stuck along the cable. Using the bosun's chair and pulley system set up in each car, the patrollers and tramway employees lowered passengers through the trapdoors of the tramcars. Everyone arrived safely to the ground and walked down the mountain to the Valley Station.[106] That the evacuation was conducted smoothly and without a single injury is testament to the early organization of the Cannon Mountain operation.

Before the advent of snowmaking systems and snow grooming equipment, the ski patrol at Cannon also served as the trail maintenance crew. They filled in ruts and "sitzmarks," the large divots left behind by fallen skiers, with the binary goal of creating a positive skiing experience and preventing injuries. For many years, the weekly time trials on the Cannon Trail were run on Wednesdays, and the ski patrol spent considerable time preparing for the race. "Usually after a weekend, we started in Monday morning fixing all the trails so they'd be in shape to ski again," said Boothroyd. "We worked Monday and Tuesday shoveling all the way down the whole two miles and a third" of the trail.[107]

Before the advent of snowcats and groomers, Cannon patrollers rigged snow rollers from wooden slats, about five feet long, connecting two bicycle-sized wheels and attached to long toboggan-type handles. Patrollers lined up in overlapping paths and pulled the heavy, cumbersome contraptions behind them to smooth out some of the bumps and ruts along the trails.[108] Bob Ball, a member of the Cannon patrol in the 1950s, remembers that patroller Bob Finn once lost control of a roller near the bottom of the Taft Trail and simply let it go: "He said, 'I never wanted to do this again, and I never wanted anyone else to do it,' and he headed it right into the woods…That was the end of the roller."[109]

By the mid-1950s, snow cats were on the scene at Cannon, improving the mountain's grooming ability. While there was a grooming crew that worked during the day, patrollers often drove snow cats for nighttime grooming. The first cats at Cannon were Bombardiers, but the tracks weren't wide enough for winter grooming. Next came the Tucker Sno-Cat, with pontoons and steel tracks, which could pull a roller or chain link fence to break up the ice and smooth the snow. These early cats were only powerful enough to groom when pointed down the hill. "When we were getting a blizzard, we'd just

An early Tucker Sno-Cat pulls a grooming device near the Banshee slopes at Cannon, circa mid-1950s. *Charles Trask photo, NESM Collection.*

try to keep a single road [cleared] to the top of the tram so we could get up there," said Jere Peabody. Peabody recalled the frightening thrill of his first time grooming the steep Zoomer Trail in a Tucker Sno-Cat when he was following Kirman Pineo, who was on the grooming crew at Cannon for years: "When you tipped over and started down the Zoomer, there was no stopping. Those things would turn so fast, you had no control anymore. You just had to go straight."[110]

Many Cannon characters have come through the ski patrol since 1938, and many have served on the patrol for decades. Since its inception, the patrol has had only seven directors. Ken Boothroyd left during World War II, when the mountain staff was cut significantly, but he returned to work as a weekend patroller for more than twenty years. After the war, Austin Macauley, known by his crew as "Sonny" or "Mac," took over as head of the ski patrol. Macauley was also a naturalist and avid photographer, and he was involved in much of the early work to preserve the Old Man of the Mountain. Mickey Libby became director in 1972, after more than twenty years on patrol at

The Cannon Mountain Ski Patrol in the late 1940s included, from left, patrol chief Austin "Sonny" Macauley, Wesley Talbot, Bob Finn, Roger Peabody, Don Eastman, Jim Dudley and Bob Ball. *Charles Trask photo, NESM Collection.*

Cannon, and remained in the position until his retirement in 1989. Mickey was a friend to generations of Cannon skiers and was as much an ambassador for the mountain as he was ski patrol boss. He was followed by Mike Pelchat, Jack Harrison, Gareth Slattery (now operations manager at Cannon) and Bill Mead, who started on patrol in 1968 and became director in 2006.

Cannon patrollers were involved in 1962 in organizing the Professional Ski Patrol Association (PSPA) to develop professional standards and examinations for ski patrollers. Several Cannon ski patrollers have served as examiners for PSPA, including Larry Collins in the association's early days.[111] Collins also served as PSPA president and helped establish the western division of PSPA. The organization presents an annual Larry Collins Award in his memory, given for either a particularly admirable deed or in honor of longstanding contributions to ski patrolling.[112]

Cannon ski patrollers have always prided themselves on being professionals on the hill, but they also like to kid around within their own ranks. Jere Peabody's lunchbox was once epoxied shut by his patrol colleagues and left in his nailed-closed locker. Charlie Miller, a longtime patroller at Cannon and a favorite among his peers, was known as a packrat. "Charlie was always picking up things at lost and found, and first of the season Mac would always get a box of wax and files…Charlie was always taking one or two extra, always had them in his locker," recalled Rich Millen, who started on patrol in 1955 and remained on weekend duty for nearly three decades. "So, one day we cut a strip right down through [his locker], and put in Plexiglas. Just like a thermometer—you could look and see what he had in there."[113]

In the 1960s, when patrollers weren't out on the hill helping fallen skiers or trying to smooth a trail, they were often embroiled in fierce cribbage competitions. Every patrol station on the mountain had a cribbage board—generally homemade from an old ski—until assistant mountain manager Newt Avery, fed up with the distraction, threw them out one day. After that, patrollers became more creative, and cribbage boards were drilled into the bottoms of benches and chairs so the competitions could continue.

Today's patrollers carry on the cribbage tradition, the pranks and the professionalism. "The only thing that's changed [on Cannon's patrol] since I came in 1968 is the people," said Mead. "The camaraderie and how we do business is all the same. It's a tightknit group."[114]

SEL HANNAH AND SNO-ENGINEERING

It was Otto Schniebs, legendary Dartmouth ski coach and professor of all things skiing, who said, "Skiing is more than a sport—it is a way of life." That mantra was particularly true for Selden "Sel" Hannah, who raced for Schniebs's Dartmouth team in the early 1930s, built a career around skiing and influenced the development of hundreds of ski areas. Some of Hannah's earliest work was laying out many of the first trails on Cannon Mountain, which he could see from his home in nearby Sugar Hill. In 1958, along with a few of the regular guests at his Ski Hearth Farm, Hannah established Sno-engineering, setting the foundation for what has become the premier ski area design firm, certainly in the United States and perhaps in the world. In its more than fifty-year history, Sno-engineering—now SE Group—has designed ski areas and resorts across the globe and has included the work of such principals as Ted Farwell and Jim Branch, both members (along with Hannah) of the U.S. National Ski Hall of Fame, and Joe Cushing, who has likely had a hand in designing more ski trails than anyone.

Sel Hannah filled myriad roles in his lifetime—ski patroller, ski lodge host, poet, partyer, would-be Olympian, farmer, teacher of army ski troops and ski area designer. He was "uncommonly talented, inexhaustible and just plain tough,"[115] but he also loved to spin a yarn on most any subject and could dance "the polka around the living room and up on the sofa and over the chairs."[116] Hannah grew up immersed in the Nordic skiing tradition of the historic Nansen Ski Club in Berlin, New Hampshire. His first pair of skis—probably jumping skis—was strapped to his feet nearly as soon as he

Sel Hannah, circa 1940s. *NESM Collection*.

could walk, and he learned to ski in the woods behind his family's home and along the logging roads crisscrossing the forests of the Berlin area.

From jumping, he progressed to cross-country and eventually to alpine skiing. He became proficient in all forms and as a boy took to climbing the Mount Washington carriage road on skis and schussing his way home.[117] He achieved myriad racing accolades, in both Nordic and Alpine events, from his time on the Dartmouth ski team through senior competitions decades later. Hannah was named to the 1940 U.S. Olympic Nordic Ski Team, although the Olympics were not held that year due to World War II. He was active in the local Franconia Ski Club for much of his life, helping to host races and develop the club's junior program.

Hannah dabbled in ski trail construction during the 1930s. He was on the work crew that, directed by Schniebs, built the aptly named Hell's Highway trail on Mount Moosilauke in 1933. That year, Sel also placed fifth in the first National Downhill, held on Moosilauke's carriage road. In 1936, he laid out the Tecumseh trail to be cut by the Civilian Conservation Corps at what would, three decades later and under the direction of Hannah and Sno-engineering, become the Waterville Valley ski area. By the time Cannon's Tramway opened, Hannah had developed enough of a reputation as a trail builder that when he and his bride, Paulie Lee, happened by the tramway in the summer of 1938 to check out the new contraption, Roland Peabody hired him "on the spot to supervise the construction of the ski trails" being built on Cannon by the CCC.[118] Hannah worked designing and cutting trails at Cannon and on the ski patrol there until World War II, when he spent a short time as ski instructor to army paratroops in Utah.

Sel and Paulie Hannah purchased a farm in Sugar Hill, with clear views of Cannon and the Franconia Range. They moved in the day before the hurricane of '38 roared through the valley, partially flooding the farm and farmhouse and downing much of the property's timber. The September storm also wreaked havoc on the newly laid out Cannon trails, creating wind problems that in some areas still exist. "The trails were a mess. One large section about mid-mountain where I had designed the Cannon trail through high timber, which I hoped would act as a wind [screen,] was completely blown down," Sel wrote in his notes. The job of connecting the two portions of that trail, which had been started before Hannah's arrival—the top by ski patrol chief Ken Boothroyd, the bottom by trail builder Charley Proctor—was already "impossible." CCC workers who had been cutting the trail were moved for a time to clearing the highways, which the storm had rendered impassable.[119]

Around Sel's shifts at the mountain, the Hannahs tended a small herd of cows, developed a milk route and eventually created a truck farm that delivered vegetables to area grocers and restaurants and was renowned for its potatoes. They also raised four children, all skillful skiers. During the winter months, they took in boarders at Ski Hearth Farm, providing rustic bunk room accommodations, breakfast, a trail lunch, dinner served family style at a long table and plenty of merriment for the bargain price of $3.50 per day. "The guests were friendly and many interesting," Sel wrote years later. "We spent long evenings discussing philosophies…skiing, racing, and love."[120] Some of the guests at Ski Hearth Farm would later collaborate with Sel to form Sno-Engineering. Some of his farmhands—namely Joe Cushing and Ford Hubbard—developed into adept trail designers and spent many decades with the company.

After the war, there was a demand for more ski trails and bigger ski areas, and Hannah went "whole hog" into the business of designing these. He was familiar with the mountains from hiking them in all seasons—in winter to ski, and in other seasons to hunt and explore. He knew the contours of the land, the direction of the winds and the gullies that might catch and hold snow. "He was most at home while 'on the mountain,'" said one business partner. "He was able, beyond any other person, to visualize the finished product while standing in the midst of densely packed conifers or a river of boulders and to forever impact the ski industry as we know it."[121]

With a combination of mountain wisdom, a respect for the land and what his daughter Joan calls "farmer logic," Hannah honed his trail design skills, using the natural features of a mountain to create "attractive, flowing, rhythmic, fun ski trails."[122] He incorporated erosion control techniques into his work and began to contemplate the many attributes beyond trail design that ski areas would need. Other skiers were thinking about the growing industry as well. A few "wealthy people who wanted something to do with skiing"[123] and who were regular guests at Ski Hearth Farm, some with engineering backgrounds, banded together in the late 1950s. They recruited Hannah to handle the trail design aspect of the company, and Sno-engineering was born.

The founders included Hannah, Bill Shaw, David Heald and William Walsh. Shaw, an avid skier and longtime guest at Ski Hearth Farm with experience in the construction business, became president of the fledgling company. Heald's background ranged from advertising and hotel management to equipment sales and service. He was treasurer and advisor for Sno-engineering. Walsh, a chemical engineer with experience in the snowmaking business, served as executive vice-president and general manager. The founders planned to offer site location for potential ski areas, layout and design for trails and lifts, lift engineering, snowmaking recommendations, facilities planning and promotion and advertising services.[124]

In 1965, Hannah took complete control of Sno-engineering, setting up the office in the Ski Hearth farmhouse, which until the mid-1950s had boarded skiers. By the time he took over, Hannah had enlisted Joe Cushing and Ted Farwell to join the company.

Cushing was a longtime Cannon skier who moved to Sugar Hill after graduating from college. He and his wife, Mary, purchased a two-hundred-year-old farmhouse across the Gale River from Ski Hearth Farm, where Cushing had worked since his college summers. When Sel had lots of trail design work, he'd pull Cushing out of the fields to help.[125] Cushing was a quick study and became "as good a trail and slope and area layout man as there is in the country," according to Hannah. "Our designs are so much alike that I can go into an area that he's been in, unknown to me, and when we come out and compare what we've done afterwards we'll have laid out almost identical systems."[126]

Sno-engineering founder Sel Hannah (left) pauses outside the office with neighbor and longtime Sno-engineering trail designer Joe Cushing in the 1960s. *Courtesy Joe Cushing.*

Joe Cushing spent more than three decades with Sno-engineering, working on between four and five hundred projects, with perhaps two hundred reaching fruition as ski resorts. Among his favorite projects, Cushing counts two very different ski areas. One is the quintessential resort of Deer Valley, Utah, which he worked on from the 1970s until his retirement in 1995, when he handed the reins over to his son Chris, who remains a principal at SE Group. The other is Mount Wachusett, a Massachusetts ski area boasting a mere one thousand vertical feet of skiing. Wachusett is where, in the 1940s, a teenaged Joe Cushing skied to the Massachusetts Junior Downhill title on an old trail not more than twenty feet wide. Years later, with Sno-engineering, he would build a ski area there, "practically from scratch."[127]

Farwell was a three-time Olympian and former National Cross-Country Ski Champion with an MBA from Stanford University. He remained with Sno-engineering, becoming part owner and in 1969 opening a branch office in Colorado, until leaving the company in 1972 to launch his own consulting firm.[128] To the design skills of Hannah and Cushing, Farwell added much-needed financial and marketing expertise. The company's work during the 1960s included trail designs at nearby Loon Mountain and Waterville Valley.

In 1967, Jim Branch joined the company, becoming president and part owner two years later, when the Hannah family sold all stock in Sno-engineering. Hannah would remain actively involved in ski area design, as an independent consultant, right up until his death in 1991—more than a half century of building ski trails at more than 250 areas. But in 1969, with the ski industry entering a boom, Sno-engineering was posed for great growth, and Hannah was looking for a lighter workload.

Branch had been managing the fledgling Alyeska resort in Alaska for seven years and wanted to relocate with his young family to more moderate climes. He and Joe Cushing had been college roommates at Dartmouth (which Cushing attended briefly), and Sno-engineering seemed a good fit for Branch. He had an MBA from Dartmouth's Tuck School of Business, an on-the-job understanding of starting and managing a ski area and a lifelong love of skiing. He had raced for the Dartmouth ski team, served in the army as a ski patrolman stationed in Garmisch, Germany, and worked on the ski patrol at Colorado's Loveland Basin before taking on the task of opening Alyeska.[129]

Jim Branch, who became president of Sno-engineering in 1969, surveys a project. *Courtesy Phil Branch.*

Branch was energetic, bright and passionate about skiing and his work within the resort industry. With an "encyclopedic knowledge and broad experience" in the resort planning field, he became widely respected at ski resorts everywhere and regularly acted as lecturer and expert panelist.[130] Olympian and Waterville Valley developer Tom Corcoran called Branch "a messiah, a prophet who could be the conscience of the ski industry and its critic because he knew so much about it and was such a proponent."[131]

Branch remained at the helm of Sno-engineering until his death in 1991, guiding the ski area design company Sel Hannah had founded into the premier mountain resort planning company in the world, with projects across North America and as far-flung as Asia and Scandinavia. "He was very proud that he got to go places like New Zealand and Czechoslovakia and South Africa to sort of promote skiing and help other countries get started," said his wife, Peg Branch. His favorite projects included a small ski area in southern Pennsylvania—Whitetail Resort—which opened just after his death, and the renowned Deer Valley, which Sno-engineering helped create and grow over more than two decades.[132]

Sno-engineering evolved from a company that mainly designed ski trails into one that helped create year-round mountain resorts, covering every aspect from market analysis and environmental impact to construction management and marketing. By 1990, the company had completed some fifteen hundred resort projects and was working on forty or fifty jobs at any given time. Sno-engineering had a staff of more than thirty, a main office in Littleton, New Hampshire, and branch offices scattered across the country and abroad.[133]

Past associates of Sno-engineering have gone on to such ventures as overseeing planning for the Aspen Ski Company and running Booth Creek Ski Holdings. Some, like Cushing and Ford Hubbard, spent many years with Sno-engineering. Hubbard had worked on Sel and Paulie Hannah's farm in the 1960s. He grew up in Franconia and learned to ski at Cannon Mountain, then served a stint for the army in Alaska. He was a skiing star at Franconia's Dow Academy, worked for the Cannon ski patrol and in the early 1960s was on the National Biathlon Team.

In 1964, Hubbard returned to New Hampshire and worked periodically for Sno-engineering until 1982, when he joined the company full time, working on snowmaking systems and the design and construction of both cross-country and alpine trails. He had a hand in the design of over forty resorts and planned the biathlon and cross-country facilities for the 1988 Calgary Olympics.[134] Hubbard also designed some of the newer trail and lift development at Cannon Mountain, including the collection of beginner and intermediate trails that opened around the Tuckerbrook Chairlift in 2003.[135]

Through the course of its history, Sno-engineering has transformed continually to keep up with the changes in the ski industry. The company has helped develop numerous resorts throughout the continent, from Stratton and Okemo in Vermont to Maine's Sugarloaf, from glamorous Aspen and remote Crested Butte in Colorado to the cowboy country turned upscale resort towns of Jackson Hole, Wyoming, and Steamboat Springs, Colorado. Canadian projects include historic Mont Tremblant in Quebec Province and sprawling Whistler in British Columbia.[136] Now doing business as SE Group, the company has offices in Vermont, Colorado, Utah and Washington State and offers services from resort planning and environmental assessment to landscape architectural planning.

It all started on a farm with a view of Cannon Mountain and a man who loved skiing and the wildness of the mountains. "I've tried…to keep the essence and the character of the trails, so they're a great deal more like the old-fashioned trails," Hannah said in 1979 of his ski area design efforts. "It's really a lovely thing, a beautiful life."[137] Through his vision, and that of the people who have followed—Joe Cushing, Ford Hubbard, Jim Branch and others—skiers everywhere have found a bit of that beautiful life. It is in the exhilaration of arcing turns down the fall line, gliding along trails that unfurl from a summit, the splendor of simply being on the mountain in winter.

WARTIME SKIING AND POST–WORLD WAR II DEVELOPMENT

As the winter of 1941–42 began, American skiing was flourishing, and Franconia had emerged as a premier ski center. Anchored by Cannon Mountain, many surrounding towns offered rope tows and ski jumps, ice-skating rinks and tobogganing hills to add to the region's wintertime appeal. Cannon skiers had uphill transportation via the tram and the new Alpine lift T-bar at the top of the mountain, which provided skiers access to the uppermost trails without having to descend the entire mountain each run. The Taft Slalom, Cannon, Ravine and brand-new Hardscrabble Trails spiraled down from the summit. Those willing to hike over the saddle could ski Coppermine, Tucker Brook and the Taft Racecourse. A practice slope near the Valley Station provided a more open area for beginners to improve their skills. Trains arrived each weekend from Boston and New York carrying eager skiers, who found plenty of ski lodges around Franconia for after-skiing festivities and nighttime accommodations. Then came the United States' entry into World War II, and everything changed.

Prominent skiers throughout the country enlisted in the armed services, many to serve as ski troops. Others joined the war effort as factory workers. Gas rations, altered train schedules and a changed economy meant that people were not always free to travel and spend their days sliding down snow-covered trails. At the same time, there was a focus on physical fitness as a matter of national pride and readiness to serve the country, and skiing was promoted as a way to stay fit. When the war ended four years later, American skiing experienced significant growth. State-owned Cannon could not keep pace, and the mountain tumbled from its early glory years into a slump, falling behind emerging ski areas in Vermont and the western United States. It wasn't until the mid-1950s that Cannon made the improvements it needed to remain relevant in the increasingly competitive ski scene, and then it was an ongoing struggle to catch up and keep up.

In January 1942, just a month after the attack on Pearl Harbor, the Tramway Commission decided to keep the mountain open, reasoning that "continued operation of the tramway will be in accord with the national program of physical fitness."[138] There was a call around the nation for Americans to take their recreation with the war effort in mind, and President Franklin D. Roosevelt urged citizens to use leisure time patriotically, "with the purpose of building up body and mind and with the chief thought that this will help win the war."[139]

This focus on healthy recreation, combined with travel restrictions, led to a reawakening of ski touring trails around Cannon. Although the popular snow trains were cancelled during the war, skiers continued to arrive by regular rail service to nearby Littleton or more distant depots. From train stations, they were transported to Cannon via ski lodge hosts with station wagons or on a bus running through the Notch. After a day on the mountain, many visitors skied back to their lodges, affording Franconia "the appearance of a European ski village."[140]

Despite the challenges of getting to Franconia, Cannon remained a popular destination during the war. Newspapers and magazines as varied as the Boston-based *Ski Bulletin*, *Time* and *Mademoiselle* featured articles and photo spreads of the Franconia ski scene. The Franconia Notch Area association—a kind of chamber of commerce for the region—reported in April 1942 that "the Area" had garnered some $51,000 of free publicity during the winter, including mentions in 166 newspapers and twelve magazines and on eleven radio stations.[141] Area inns and hotels were filled nearly to capacity, and the tram boasted greater numbers of skiers in December 1941 than it had the previous year. Local skiers Sel Hannah, Hans Thorner and Alec Behr formed a new ski school to serve skiers clamoring for instruction. "It looks as though people are going to ski if they can do nothing else," wrote ski columnist Tap Goodenough in the *Boston Evening American*.[142]

By February, however, most of the instructors around Franconia, along with many tramway employees, had enlisted in the army or gone to work in war factories. Cannon's staff was diminished from about thirty-five employees to a skeleton crew of eight, and most of the skiers riding the tram were servicemen or defense workers and their families. More than

Franconia Notch Winter Sports, New Hampshire

10 percent of Franconia's six hundred inhabitants joined the service.[143] Sel Hannah headed west with Dick Durrance, Walter Prager and other skiing greats to teach skiing to a battalion of paratroopers. Franconia instructors Peter Gabriel and Alec Behr ended up in the now legendary 10th Mountain

This 1941 map shows the array of winter activities available in the Franconia area. Many towns had rope tows, skating rinks and other entertainment. *Author's collection.*

Division, along with Franconia skier Bob Ball and Joel Coffin III, who was among the many fatalities of the 10th in its fighting in the Italian Alps.

Alec Bright, Norwood Ball, Bobby Clark (who was killed in action), Bernard and Bertram Herbert and many other Cannon skiers joined the

Alec Behr, Sel Hannah and Swiss skier Hans Thorner in 1941. Behr served in the 10th Mountain Division. Hannah trained paratroops to ski in Utah. Thorner taught skiing in Franconia for several years and later founded Magic Mountain in Vermont. *NESM Collection.*

service, as did Dr. Jim Bogle, who through his work with the Cannon Ski Patrol before the war had become "an expert with broken bones." The *Concord Monitor & New Hampshire Patriot* claimed, "Cannon Mountain has become a training ground for the army ski troops…Every day there are more boys who come to ski and train—not for fun—but to keep in condition before they go to ski for Uncle Sam."[144] Soon, only a few—including Swiss instructor Hans Thorner, who also ran a ski lodge, and Sig Buchmayr— were left to teach skiing in Franconia. For a time, the Austrian Buchmayr was detained as an "enemy alien," although he was released soon before his wife gave birth to their triplet sons in January 1942 at Littleton Hospital.[145]

With the end of the war in 1945, many local skiers returned to Franconia. Others wandered away from Cannon to other work or other ski areas. Some, of course, never came home from the war. Cannon continued, for a few years, to be a leading ski area. In 1946, the first U.S. National Alpine Championships since 1942 were held on the Taft, in conjunction with the annual Hochgebirge races. The event was a meeting of the old and the new. It was among the last big races to be held on the country's first race trail and included several World War II veterans from all over the country, who had played an important role in the early days of American skiing. "It was really great to sort of get the old gang together again," said Norwood Ball, who had skied the Taft since he was a kid and was a war veteran at the time of the 1946 races. "Of course about this time a lot of new, younger skiers were coming along and doing a really good job."[146]

A lot of new, younger ski areas were coming along in those postwar years, too, and they soon unseated Cannon as a top dog in the ski world. In the late 1940s, Cannon expanded its practice slope (today known as Banshee), extended the rope tow there and built a tiny warming hut at the bottom of the open slope. The mountain also added a few new trails. But those small changes, the funding for which had to be approved by the state legislature, proved too little to keep pace with the rapid growth of skiing in the Northeast.

While before the war Cannon had been at the forefront of ski area development—with trail building, racing, the tramway, the ski patrol and promotion of the area as a skiing mecca—by the late 1940s, "New Hampshire [had] reverted to its historic stance of Yankee conservatism, so that after World War II there were fewer state resources directed toward skiing."[147] This conservative approach meant it took longer for Cannon to acquire the amenities necessary to operate a successful ski area in an increasingly competitive market. While the adjacent Mittersill Ski Area, opened in 1945, introduced snowmaking in the early 1950s, for instance, Cannon was completely reliant on natural snow until 1969, when the state allowed the purchase of a $544,000 snowmaking system.[148]

To further complicate the process of bringing change and necessary state funding to Cannon, the state abolished the Aerial Tramway Commission in 1950, and management of the ski area and Franconia Notch State Reservation was transferred to what would become the State Division of Parks. The Tramway Commission had overseen the skiing operation at Cannon since the construction of the tramway in 1937 and had included members from the North Country who understood the region and Cannon's importance to the local economy and who worked to help the ski area develop as needed to remain viable. "Somehow in the shuffle, the direction passed back to Concord and…Franconia as a major ski complex started to slide," wrote Sel Hannah years later.[149]

Roland Peabody's death in 1950 meant that Cannon Mountain also lost one of its longest and strongest proponents and a great local diplomat who

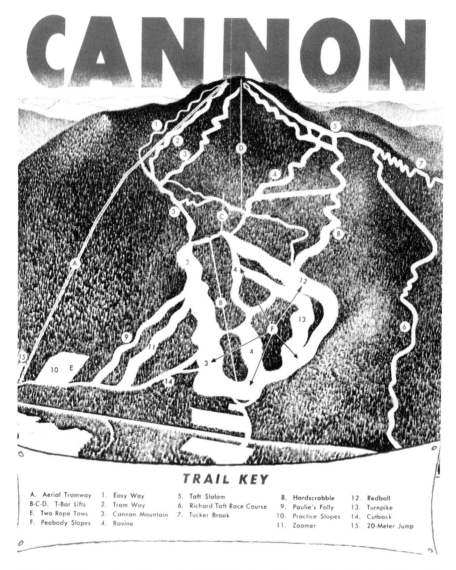

TRAIL KEY

A. Aerial Tramway	1. Easy Way	5. Taft Slalom
B-C-D. T-Bar Lifts	2. Tram Way	6. Richard Taft Race Course
E. Two Rope Tows	3. Cannon Mountain	7. Tucker Brook
F. Peabody Slopes	4. Ravine	

8. Hardscrabble	12. Redball
9. Paulie's Folly	13. Turnpike
10. Practice Slopes	14. Cutback
11. Zoomer	15. 20-Meter Jump

This mid-1950s map shows Cannon's original ski trails and the new Roland Peabody Memorial Slopes, as well as the Taft Race Course and the Tucker Brook trail. *NESM Collection.*

had been respected by both the mountain employees and the legislators who ultimately made the decisions that would affect Cannon's growth as a ski area. The focus for Franconia Notch shifted away from skiing and to the broader realm of year-round recreation. As in the past, any profits from operations within Franconia Notch were absorbed into the state's budget and redistributed as legislators saw fit, with only a portion of surplus revenue used for improvements at Cannon and other Notch attractions.[150]

By the mid-1950s, it was clear that Cannon either needed to make changes or get out of the ski business. "Skiing facilities at Cannon are virtually still through the woods on a narrow trail basis which has become antiquated during the war," Alec Bright told state legislators in 1953. "Unless somebody brings about the development of up-ski facilities and opens up the terrain…you don't stand a chance to regain the prestige that you ought to have."[151] The tramway remained the only way, save climbing on foot or ski, to access trails from the valley floor. Sometimes the wind was too strong to run the tram. Sometimes the weather at the top—or condition of the trails—was too brutal for all but the hardiest skiers. And sometimes the line was just too long to merit waiting.

John Carleton, long a champion of skiing in Franconia, found himself in a particularly lengthy procession at the Tram's Valley Station one February day in 1950 and resorted to climbing the mountain to keep a ski date. He complained of the incident to Governor Sherman Adams (who would develop the nearby Loon Mountain ski area in the 1960s) and was subsequently appointed chairman of a committee to study potential solutions to Cannon's skiing woes.[152] The improvements recommended by

The Peabody base area and T-bar, circa late 1960s. The right ell of the 1953 base lodge was added in 1963. The T-bar ran from the winter of 1954 until it was replaced by the "Hong Kong" chair in 1972. *Bromley & Co. postcard, NESM collection.*

Carleton's committee were rejected by the state legislature in 1951. But in 1953, legislators approved a $305,000 expansion project that would be the first step in modernizing Cannon's skiing facilities.

The project included improving existing trails, constructing a base lodge with a cafeteria and warming facilities, building a new parking area and creating five new "boulevard trails" designed by Sel Hannah: Red Ball, Lower Cannon, Turnpike, Zoomer and Lower Ravine. Two new T-bars were installed, and skiers could now reach the summit by riding the new lower T-bar, then the new middle T-bar and finally the existing Alpine lift T-bar.[153] Named in honor of Cannon's founding father, the Roland Peabody Memorial Slopes were ready for action at the start of the 1953–4 winter. When there was finally enough snow to open the new lifts in late January 1954, the boost to Cannon skiing was immediately apparent. The ski area realized record numbers of skiers (four thousand) and gross income of $6,406 (more than $2,000 higher than the previous two-day record) that first weekend.[154]

Still, skiing at Cannon and around New Hampshire continued to lag for a time. By 1960, New Hampshire had fourteen major ski areas—with only eight open on weekdays—and an uphill capacity (on weekends) of roughly twenty-four thousand skiers per hour. Vermont skiing, meanwhile, was cruising, with twenty-three major ski areas and an uphill capacity of more than fifty-two thousand skiers per hour—more than double that of New Hampshire.[155]

Franconia-area residents and business leaders continued to lobby for improvements at Cannon. "By the time the Peabody Slopes were finally created to fill the need of the '40s, it was 1953 and they were already inadequate," wrote Sel Hannah in a 1961 report for the State Planning and Development Commission.[156] In the early 1960s, the state approved and funded some improvements: many of the mid-mountain trails were widened to create better flow from the upper to the lower sections of the mountain, new trails were cut on the Route 3 side of Cannon and the mountain's first chairlifts were installed. (By comparison, Mount Snow in Vermont had opened in 1955 with two new chairlifts and plans to install five more for the following ski season.)[157]

As other New Hampshire areas like Loon and Waterville Valley were developed in the mid-1960s, skiers traveling north from Boston often pulled off the highway before reaching Cannon. Those who made it as far as Franconia Notch found what *Skiing* magazine writer (and North Country resident) John Jerome described in 1969 as "rollicking, old-fashioned, un-super-groomed" skiing.[158]

Cannon has come a long way since those days and has garnered industry accolades for value, accessibility, amazing scenery and challenging terrain. It has also retained its notoriety as a cold, windy "skier's mountain." Through Cannon's many years as a ski area, the folks who run the mountain have often tried to reinvent its image, alternately embracing and refuting Cannon's rugged reputation. When the practice slope was cut by the Valley Station in 1939, offering gentler terrain than the original top-to-bottom trails, Cannon called itself a "family area." It made the claim again with the creation of the Peabody slopes in 1953 and with the development of the Tuckerbrook Family Area fifty years later.

The reality is that Cannon is both things: a skier's mountain *and* a family area. Sometimes the skiing at Cannon is on the gentle, open, "family" slopes. Sometimes it's through the woods, in the old style Alec Bright lamented back in 1953 but which many have come to cherish the more skiing has changed. Generations of "Cannon kids" have grown up on the mountain's slopes, including a number of Olympians. In learning to ski at Cannon, they become skilled enough to ski anywhere. Often, however, the place they really want to be is back on the home hill. *Skiing*'s Jerome put it this way: "People who love Cannon love it with a passion that is hard to explain to…skiers who have become accustomed to having mountains made easy for them. Cannon has texture. You might even call it character."[159]

MITTERSILL

The Austrian Baron and His Ski Village Dream

W hen Austrian Baron Hubert von Pantz arrived in Franconia in April 1939, it was love at first sight. He reached town—road weary and via a two-hundred-mile, twenty-five-dollar taxi ride from snowless Lake Placid—to find a Swiss ski instructor dressed in Tyrolean garb outside the picturesque Lovett's Inn. The next morning, he discovered on Cannon Mountain both the tramway and a parade of Easter "ski bunnies…[whose] gay costumes…made the mountainside glow in all colors of the rainbow."[160] The mountains of Franconia Notch reminded him of his homeland, which he had fled during the Nazi Anschluss. Newly arrived in the United States, with a title of European nobility but little money, the baron dreamed of creating an Austrian ski village, complete with slopeside chalets, a charming inn and all the niceties an elegant clientele would demand.

"I fell in love with New Hampshire on the spot," von Pantz wrote in his autobiography nearly half a century after his arrival in Franconia. "I knew exactly where I wanted to build my dream village: in New Hampshire, where I had spent my first weekend after my arrival in the States and which had reminded me so much of my own beloved Austrian Alps."[161] Within a year of coming to America, the baron had purchased some five hundred acres of land adjacent to Cannon Mountain, although it would be five years before he succeeded in opening his Mittersill ski area. Mittersill enjoyed glory days through the 1950s and '60s and then suffered a long decline and eventual closure in 1984. Its history has become intertwined with Cannon's, through its personalities, its evolution as a ski area, its very trails, and its revival as part of the Cannon Mountain operation.

Baron Hubert von Pantz.
NESM Collection.

Mittersill U.S.A. was not the baron's first foray into running a resort. In 1934, with a group of friends, he had purchased Schloss Mittersill, "a medieval castle directly out of a fairytale, perched on top of a mountain… overlooking the snowcapped Austrian Alps."[162] The exclusive club catered to the very wealthy, offering hunting and fishing, a sauna and massage rooms, horseback riding and skiing. Millionaires from America and nobles from several European countries were members at Schloss Mittersill, until the Nazis occupied Austria and the castle during World War II.

The baron was at home in an elite crowd. Born in the early part of the twentieth century to a family that had made its fortune through ownership of iron mines in Europe and had been titled since the 1400s, the baron was raised in the Austrian countryside and schooled in Vienna. With the fall of the Austrian Empire after World War I, the fortunes of the von Pantz family and many others dwindled, but the titles held fast.

While his family had lost much of its fortune, the baron retained his charm. With the dominating demeanor of someone raised among nobility

Hubert von Pantz (left) with his brother, Kurt von Pantz, and Cristina de Bourbon Patino at a Franconia Ski Club dance in the 1940s. *Enzo Serafini Collection.*

and a good dose of conviviality, the baron kept his guests at Schloss Mittersill happily entertained. He used the same charm to woo, by his own account, a string of wealthy women that included legendary fashion designer Coco Channel, Aileen Plunkett of the Guinness clan, and former queens and countesses. "I did have a great many affairs, too many probably, for I simply could not resist a beautiful face," von Pantz wrote in his autobiography.[163] Some of these women helped finance the baron's business initiatives, and one—Cristina de Bourbon Patino, a Spanish princess by birth and the estranged wife to a Bolivian tin heir—provided some of the funding for the baron to bring his dream of a ski village to life in the mountains of New Hampshire.[164]

In 1940, for a price of $1,350, Baron von Pantz purchased 550 acres on Mount Jackson, at the edge of Cannon Mountain, from a local logging company.[165] The property was bordered by state park and National Forest Service land, a location that offered incredible beauty and immediate solitude. With Cannon's trails and tramway just around the corner, the spot was "a veritable skiers' paradise." The baron set to work planning his ski village and promoting what was to come. He was joined in his efforts by his countryman Sig Buchmayr, already a favorite instructor and skiing personality in the area. "The atmosphere of the Austrian Tyrol will be transplanted to the White Mountains of New Hampshire in the Franconia Mittersill," predicted the *Manchester Union* in an article that described a Mittersill that, when completed, would include a "main chateau" with private accommodations, dormitory units, a cafeteria, shops, private chalets, a "Stube" and yodelers providing entertainment. Von Pantz expected to be in operation by the following winter.[166]

In the meantime, the baron rented the Sunset Hill House annex in Sugar Hill and began welcoming guests of the same caliber he'd entertained at Schloss Mittersill: big city socialites and uber-wealthy Europeans who had left the war at home to come to America. Among his earliest ski guests were Barbara Hutton, then one of the world's richest women, Danish count Curt Haugwitz-Reventlow, Jack Heinz of the Heinz 57 family, and members of the literary Hemmingway clan.[167] Sig offered ski instruction on the slopes of the golf course at Sunset, not far from his previous instruction venue at Peckett's, or brought clients to the more challenging trails on Cannon. All the while, the baron planned his ski village in the mountains. Alas, red tape and the United States' entry into World War II interrupted Mittersill's creation. A property dispute with the state prevented the baron from building an access road to the site of Mittersill until a neighbor gave him a right of way through his property.[168] The war put a halt on nearly everything.

Following World War II, the baron began construction in earnest, and Mittersill opened for the winter of 1945–6 with a rope tow and a twenty-room inn.[169] By the following season, the baron's Franconia Mittersill boasted a two-thousand-foot T-bar, a one-thousand-foot rope tow and a handful of trails for beginner and intermediate skiers. There was a warming shelter and cafeteria, lighting for night skiing and a skating rink.[170] Von Pantz had enlisted as Buchmayr's successor as ski school director another Austrian, Benno Rybizka, who had brought the popular Arlberg technique of the famous Hannes Schneider ski school to the United States from Austria nearly a decade earlier.

In the early years of his American skiing endeavor, the baron filled countless roles. He sold lift tickets, ran the T-bar and rope tow, drove snow cats and acted as the Mittersill ski patrol.[171] He also had to manage the regular maintenance and occasional emergencies related to running a ski area and hotel. One evening, the roof of the original inn blew off in a fierce New England storm, landing on the nearby power line and Mittersill's new snowplow. In the dark of a winter night, the baron and as many men as he could find at such an hour pieced together a temporary roof so that the weekend's guests would be sheltered.[172]

In the 1940s, the idea of creating a village at the base of a ski area—with lodging, dining and entertainment—was new in the United States. Within a decade, the baron would begin adding chalets at Mittersill, introducing

The original Mittersill Inn, opened in the winter of 1946, with Mount Lafayette in the background. *NESM Collection*.

the concept of financing a ski area based largely on real estate sales and rentals—an idea commonplace at modern ski areas but novel in the 1950s. The first three chalets, including one for the baron, were built in 1952. By the late 1950s, there were more than a dozen privately owned chalets, built without full kitchens to encourage the owners to dine at the Mittersill Inn.[173]

The ski village concept was one of many examples of the baron's flair for innovation and entertainment at Mittersill. In the 1950s, he installed one of the earliest snowmaking systems in New England. He had an outside bar built of ice, where lunch was served on fine days, and he organized tennis matches on the skating pond—using blue lines and red tennis balls.[174] There were skating waiters in Alpine costumes, two enormous Great Danes named Satan and Storm and a mix of guests that ranged from European princes and Hollywood stars to more typical American vacationers.

"Business and professional people rub elbows with royalty and top ranking members of American, European, and South American society in warm comradery [*sic*]," read a 1952 newspaper account of Mittersill.

An aerial view of Mittersill and Cannon ski areas from the late 1950s shows the inn and a few early chalets. The Taft Race Trail is visible above the Mittersill slopes, with a narrow trail connecting it to Mittersill. *NESM Collection.*

"Casual vacationists from Manchester or Boston who find their way into the Mittersill's well-shielded preserves are made to feel as much at home as the most publicized members of the international skiing set."[175]

Von Pantz adroitly completed a metamorphosis from ski resort jack-of-all-trades to aristocratic host to entertain his most wealthy and famous guests. Dressed for dinner in the Tyrolean jackets and pink ties of the baron's Schloss Mittersill in Austria, his entourage in Franconia regularly included royalty and Hollywood personalities, as well as some of the more well-to-do chalet owners.[176] These posh visitors—and the baron's title—did much to contribute to Mittersill's image of a swanky resort. Even before Mittersill opened, in 1941, *Harper's Bazaar* featured a photo spread of Hubert's brother, Baron Kurt von Pantz, skiing and sledding in Franconia with his wife, Sig Buchmayr and Russian prince Kyril Sherbatow and his American wife,[177] and photos and snippets of Mittersill guests appeared in the society pages of Boston and New York newspapers.

Mittersill's more moderate slopes and finished atmosphere also offered a gentle yin to Cannon's burly yang. And the baron's willingness and ability to spend money on improvements, when Cannon had to cut through the red tape of state bureaucracy, meant that Mittersill had certain things Cannon did not in the early days. Snowmaking, for instance, proved crucial for the survival of skiing in Franconia during bad snow years. "Sometimes it was watery, sometimes it was icy, but it was white," longtime Mittersill resident and photographer Dottie Crossly wrote of the early snowmaking efforts in her memoirs. With no snowmaking at Cannon in the earlier years, skiers would line up for the mellower slopes of Mittersill when necessary, just to get in some turns.

From the start, von Pantz had difficulties dealing with the state—first when he tried to build an access road into Mittersill and decades later when he sought a lease from the state to expand his ski area—but it made sense for the two areas to cooperate sometimes. Together, Mittersill and Cannon constituted one of the largest ski centers in the region in the 1960s. Occasionally, the two areas would do a joint promotion or cooperate to hold

Mittersill slopes, circa late 1950s. *Charles Trask photo, NESM Collection.*

a race, but they remained, principally, separate entities, albeit generally good neighbors. The one ongoing collaboration between the two areas for many years was ski instruction.

During the winter of 1949–50, Paul Valar took over the ski school operations at both Cannon and Mittersill, an endeavor in which he was joined by his wife, Paula Kann Valar, the following season. Paul was a past member of the Swiss ski team. Paula, Austrian by birth, had skied for the United States in the 1948 Olympics. They managed the two ski schools, along with a sport shop at Mittersill, for more than two decades. While Paul oversaw Cannon's ski school, Paula was a skillful teacher for young skiers. The moderate slopes at Mittersill were an ideal learning area, while Cannon's more expert trails were perfect for those looking for more of a challenge. Together, Cannon and Mittersill offered something for every skier.

During the 1950s, the baron traveled back to Europe several times, where he refurnished and reopened his Schloss Mittersill. During one visit to Europe, he met Terry Nichols, and the pair married in 1955—he for the first time, she for the fifth. The new baroness was American-raised, attractive and engaging, with "a strong will and boundless energy…everywhere she

The baron and his wife, Terry, celebrate New Year's Eve 1967 at Mittersill. *Dorothy Crossley photo.*

went, she was a whirlwind."[178] She was also remarkably wealthy, having inherited money from her late husbands, including the founder of the Avon Company. For the next several years, the von Pantzes spent part of their time at Mittersill and the rest at their homes in Austria and Spain or flitting around the world from one continent to the next.

Despite the ski village concept and innovations like snowmaking, the baron's ski slopes were unprofitable during the 1950s. Mittersill's ski operation averaged only about $7,000 in gross income each winter—a mere fraction of Cannon's intake. Local ski area development guru Sel Hannah appraised the Mittersill area in 1959, concluding that there was little opportunity at Mittersill for the expert and intermediate skier to find enjoyable skiing, and that the lift was "antagonizingly slow." The bordering state and national land, which provided such unspoiled beauty and peacefulness around Mittersill, also inhibited expansion of the ski area. Hannah proposed building a new lift that would extend higher on the mountain and reconfiguring the part of the famous, but decaying, Taft Race Trail that ran through Mittersill.[179]

Through the next decade, there were many changes at Mittersill. In 1960, the baron installed a new T-bar, doubling Mittersill's uphill capacity; built several more chalets; and added a thirty-unit "Gasthof" to the original inn.[180] By the late 1960s, Mittersill included more than one hundred chalets and a new inn with fifty-five guest rooms, a double chairlift and two T-bars and a fourteen-hundred-foot vertical drop with a series of new trails. One of these was Baron's Run, which incorporated part of the Taft Trail and has remained a popular run through Mittersill's downfall and rebirth.[181] The baron and Terry were spending more time in Europe and less at Mittersill U.S.A., and in the late 1960s, they sold the inn to Terry's stepson, David McConnell, and his business partner, Bob Wetenhall. A few years later, the von Pantzes sold their real estate and ski area interests to McConnell-Wetenhall as well, and Mittersill shifted "from the impassioned guidance of a titled Austrian dreamer…to the cold, bottom-line analysis of a couple of New York bankers."[182]

Without the baron's enthusiasm to buoy Mittersill, and with rising energy costs and economic inflation of the 1970s, Mittersill entered a gradual decline. In 1979, Mittersill introduced timesharing, and by 1981, the inn was completely converted from a hotel to timeshare units.[183] During the winters of 1977 and 1978, the ski slopes were opened only during weekends and holiday weeks, and during the winter of 1981–2, the slopes were closed entirely. The next two winters the resort owners, with Jack Wetenhall as president, again opened the ski slopes on weekends and holiday weeks when weather allowed.[184] The lifts finally shut down in 1984,[185] and for more than two decades, it seemed they would stay that way, the lift towers rusting away and brush growing up on the trails.

A New Hampshire forest will reclaim an untended meadow or ski trail in an amazingly short span of time, and vegetation soon encroached on Mittersill's slopes. But as the trails and lift lines became overgrown with brush and faded memories, skiers continued to hike over the saddle from Cannon to Mount Jackson, chasing powder and seeking solitude. Informal parties set out in summer months to covertly cut back the brush from some of the slopes. The old Baron's Run became a favorite "backcountry" trail, and the more adventuresome skiers had a plethora of runs to choose from—down narrow old lift lines, through secret passages and around forgotten corners.

Cannon gained the deed to the ski trails at Mittersill in 1989 for the price of one dollar,[186] but without legal access to the trails from the top of Mount Jackson, which was National Forest Service land, there was no "official" way to get to the Mittersill runs. Finally, after nearly three decades of discussion, debate and negotiation, the state and the Forest Service completed a land transfer in the spring of 2009—some 100 acres at the top of Mount Jackson for 244 acres in the Sentinel Mountain State Forest in Piermont—and Cannon was able to officially open the Mittersill trails. Hundreds of skiers turned out March 28 for the ceremonial dropping of the rope that had served as a perfunctory blockade to Mittersill for years.[187]

For the 2010–11 ski season, Cannon installed a new $3 million double chairlift along the old lift line. At a time when high-speed quad and "six-pack" chairlifts are the norm, the Mittersill double carries skiers at a more leisurely pace, allowing them to scope out their next runs and take in the awesome view of Mount Lafayette. The two-seater also ensures there is not a glut of skiers offloading simultaneously onto the Mittersill slopes on powder days. There was no snowmaking or grooming on Mittersill in 2011, and the area was operated as lift-serviced backcountry. While many area skiers decried the rebirth of Mittersill as the end of their own secret skiing stash, many others rejoiced to see the trails come alive again and looked forward to further improvements there in the future.

The inn is now owned by the Mittersill Resort Association, a trustee of the nonprofit Mittersill Alpine Resort. With fifty-three timeshare units and three hotel rooms, the resort has more than seventeen hundred owners. The Baron's Pub at the inn is a shadow of the restaurant and bar that once hosted grand dances and thrilling parties, but it is indicative of the quieter vibe surrounding Mittersill now. Next to the pub is a small case holding

A 2011 view of Mittersill, from the slopes, shows several of the more than one hundred chalets surrounding the inn. *Author photo.*

reminders of the past—a miniscule wooden chair painted in brightly colored Tyrolean flowers, old ski lift tickets and a 1951 guest register signed by "Princess Elizabeth" of Buckingham Palace. Completely separate from the inn are more than one hundred chalets, which are privately owned and are primarily vacation or seasonal homes.

The baron and his swanky friends are long gone from Mittersill, and the gatherings at the inn are smaller and more casual. Today's Mittersill, perhaps, is a far cry from what Hubert von Pantz imagined all those years ago. But the five-story Tyrolean inn, the chalets snugged into groves of birch trees along the ski trails, the joyful whoops of skiers descending through powder snow, the magnificent mountain scenery that could be New Hampshire or Austria, depending on the light and the desires of a heart—they are all pieces of what was once, simply, a baron's dream.

PAUL AND PAULA VALAR AND THE TRANSFORMATIONOF SKI INSTRUCTION

S wiss ski racer and instructor Paul Valar had his work cut out for him when he arrived in Franconia in 1949. Although Cannon was well established as a ski area—and ski instruction had been introduced at Peckett's twenty years earlier—there was no centralized ski school in Franconia. A hodgepodge of instructors had offered ski lessons around Franconia and at Cannon through the 1930s and '40s. But the ski school desk, matching instructor jackets with shiny PSIA (Professional Ski Instructors of America) pins, and a clearly labeled meeting area for students—all familiar at virtually any modern ski area—were nonexistent in skiing's early decades.

Valar was enlisted to consolidate the ski instruction efforts at Cannon and Mittersill. His able partner in this endeavor was Austrian-born ski racer Paula Kann, whom he married in 1950. The Valars ran the ski schools at the two areas for more than two decades and were indefatigable in their work to bring organization to both local and national ski instruction, as well as in their efforts to promote the Franconia area.

As Americans flocked to skiing through the early 1930s and prewar '40s, there was a growing demand for ski instruction around emerging ski centers. Peckett's-on-Sugar Hill had provided a ski school to its guests and local skiers since 1929, and other inns and ski clubs throughout the Northeast often offered some form of ski instruction. There was no means of certifying professional ski instructors, however, until 1938, and beginning skiers had no way of knowing whether the instructor they hired was the real deal or only marginally more skilled than the student. To compound the problem, some

A class in Roland Peabody's ski school warms up on the Forest Hills slope in Franconia. *Charles Trask photo, NESM Collection.*

would-be instructors charged too little for their services, undercutting the trained professionals who relied on heftier fees to make a living.[188]

In 1937, as Roland Peabody was overseeing the construction of the Cannon Mountain Aerial Tramway, the United States Eastern Amateur Ski Association (USEASA) approved a process for certifying ski instructors. The four-part certification examination included demonstration of skiing technique from downhill running to such maneuvers as jump turns and linked stem turns, ability to recognize and correct improper ski techniques, basic knowledge of first aid and an understanding of the organization of skiing from amateur rules to racing classifications. At the first exam, held in February 1938 in Woodstock, Vermont, seven of the seventeen hopefuls who participated were certified. Among them were Austrian pros Sig Buchmayr and Benno Rybizka and Swiss skier Hans Thorner, who were all connected to the Franconia ski scene at some point.[189]

In the winter of 1938–9, Roland Peabody was the chief examiner for tests held at Cannon and in Hanover, New Hampshire. That season, Franconia Ski School instructors Alec Behr, Fletcher Brown, Peter Gabriel, Louis Hechenberger and Deborah Bankhart—one of the few female instructors certified so early—passed the exam.[190] Peabody had founded his Franconia Ski School in the early 1930s but gave it up when he became tramway manager. During the 1930s and 1940s, ski instructors followed the snow around the region, often holding classes at one of the several rope tows in the area or on snow-covered golf courses or open pastures. "The school operations shifted with the weather and the snow cover," Sel Hannah recalled. "The slopes and the uphill transportation of Cannon Mountain provided no suitable place from which to operate a ski school."[191]

By the winter of 1940–1, USEASA had certified seventy-six professional instructors. Exams were not held again until after World War II.[192] Meanwhile, several instructors had set up shop in Franconia. When Peckett's ended its winter operations in 1939, the ski school there merged with Roland Peabody's Franconia Ski School, then directed by Swiss instructor Peter Gabriel.[193] Sig Buchmayr was working with Baron von Pantz and instructing under the name White Mountain Ski School.[194] Hans Thorner, who had opened his Thorner House in Franconia's Easton Valley in 1941, teamed up with locals Sel Hannah and Alec Behr to develop the Village Ski School in preparation for the winter of 1941–2.[195] When the United States entered World War II, however, all these schools were disrupted. Gabriel and Behr joined the 10th Mountain Division, Hannah went west to train parachute ski troops and Buchmayr was for a time held as an "enemy alien."

After the war, Thorner continued to offer ski lessons from his Thorner House; Buchmayr worked for a while out of the Horse & Hound Inn just down the hill from Cannon; Benno Rybizka ran the Mittersill Ski School; Roger Peabody taught under the name Profile Ski School; and Jack and Peg Kenney, at their Tamarack lodge, offered instruction to guests, as did other innkeepers. With so many instructors—some certified, some not—working on one mountain with few trails, things got a bit confusing. "We were all trying to teach skiing on the same slope," recalled Roger Peabody. "It was not infrequent, in the morning at 10:30, to find a skier coming over the hill, saying, 'I'm supposed to be in your school.' And about that time I would find someone in my class that belonged in Mr. Buchmayr's school."[196]

The confusion went beyond which ski school and instructor students were supposed to be with on a given day. Different ski teachers employed different methods of instruction based on their own backgrounds. The Arlberg technique made famous by Austrian Hannes Schneider (by this time relocated to North Conway, New Hampshire) was all the rage on ski slopes in the 1930s, but as more Europeans arrived and began teaching, they introduced Swiss and French methods. American instructors tended to compile what they found useful from the different techniques. Thus, a student might be schooled in one skiing form one weekend and an entirely different one the next. Recognizing merit in each of the various styles,

USEASA did not specify any one method for the certification process. But it was something that was frustrating to both students and ski instructors and a matter that would not be resolved until the incorporation of the Professional Ski Instructors of America (PSIA) and the American Ski Technique in the early 1960s.

Swiss-certified mountain guide and ski instructor Paul Valar was at the forefront of developing both the PSIA and the American teaching style. Raised on a dairy farm in Davos, Switzerland, Valar was a natural athlete, excelling not only in skiing but also in track and field and gymnastics. He had spent his winters on skis since the age of three, when his father crafted a homemade pair from hickory wood. He first came to the United States in the spring of 1947, at the age of twenty-seven, as a member of the Swiss National Alpine Ski Team, which trained with and raced against the U.S. team prior to the 1948 Olympics. Valar had already completed a rigorous process to become a certified Swiss ski instructor and mountain guide. He had also been the decathlon champion and four-way combined ski champion (downhill, slalom, cross-country, jumping) of his home state of Graubunden in 1946.[197] He spoke three languages fluently, but English was not one of them.

Paul and Paula Valar, circa 1950, at Mittersill. *Courtesy Christina Valar Breen.*

Luckily for Valar, one of the U.S. team members was Paula Kann, an Austrian-born skier who had come to the States to escape her Nazi-occupied country during World War II. An only child, she had grown up skiing and hiking the Alps and described her childhood self as a girl "so rugged that I could beat all the boys" at whatever the challenge—skiing, horseback riding, tennis. In the United States, Kann eventually arrived in North Conway, New Hampshire, where she trained with fellow Austrian emigrants Toni Matt and Herbert Schneider. She won the 1946 national downhill championship on Cannon's Taft Trail, adding to her long list of ski racing victories. Her training for the Olympics included hiking and skiing the headwall of Mount Washington's Tuckerman Ravine twenty-three times in the spring of 1947.[198]

Between training runs that spring, Valar and Kann, in their native German, struck up a conversation that was to last more than half a century. Valar suffered a serious neck injury just prior to the 1948 Winter Games in St. Moritz and did not compete. Battling pneumonia, Kann finished eleventh in the slalom and twenty-first in the downhill. "I didn't get an Olympic medal," she said years later. "But I got Paul."[199] During his 1947 trip to the United States with the Swiss team, Valar had also met Jack and Peg Kenney and Sel and Paulie Hannah, key players in the Franconia ski scene, who mentioned the need for a more centralized and effective ski school in Franconia. In June 1949, the board of the Franconia Ski Club, which had been founded in part

The Valars with some of their instructors during the 1950s. *From left*: Stuart Eynon, Bill Jelm, a Mr. Stackpole, Paula and Paul Valar, Ollie Cole, Ross Coffin and Stan Rowins. *Courtesy Christina Valar Breen.*

by Roland Peabody and held the rights to the name "Franconia Ski," voted unanimously to allow Valar exclusive use of the name in connection with his ski school should he decide to come to Franconia.[200]

Valar left Switzerland for the United States later that year and established on-site ski schools at Cannon and Mittersill during the winter of 1949–50. Paul and Paula were married in North Conway in 1950, honeymooned at Mittersill and then got to work. Paula had been directing the ski school at Thorn Mountain in Jackson, New Hampshire, and she brought one of her instructors, Stuie Eynon, with her to Franconia to teach, joking that he was her dowry.[201] Eynon instructed for the Valars for thirty years.

Paul and Paula weren't content to simply direct two exceptional ski schools. Over the next several years, they also ran a ski program at the White Mountain School in nearby Bethlehem, took over the ski school at state-owned Mount Sunapee and operated several ski and sport shops. In the summers, they relocated with their four daughters from the growing ski village at Mittersill to East Wallingford, Vermont, where they owned a 265-acre dairy farm. "We didn't want our daughters to grow up in a resort," Paul said. "And since I was a farmer, what the heck was I going to do in the summer? And the good part was, this way we were always independent."[202]

Their life and their work was a partnership. "Our parents were defined as a unit: Paul and Paula," said daughter Christina Valar Breen at Paul's memorial service in 2008. While Paul oversaw the ski school at Cannon, teaching advanced and expert skiers, Paula established a stellar children's ski school at Mittersill, which was featured in *Life* magazine in 1962. While Paula tended the sport shops and the couple's young family, Paul worked to restructure the way skiing was taught in the United States. "They were a team," said daughter Stefanie. "He was kind of a more professorial type… And my mother was the ultimate pragmatist. Even their skiing styles—he kind of floated along, standing tall, and you couldn't tell what the hell was going on, but he was turning. My mother had a lower stance, a much more aggressive-looking stance. She was a downhill champion. He was more elegant looking."[203]

As the ski organizers of the 1930s had perceived a need to certify ski teachers for the good of both the instructors and the students, by the 1950s there was a call among the pros to establish a method for teaching skiing and certifying instructors that would be consistent from New Hampshire to Vermont and from Minnesota to Utah to California. At the head of this charge was Paul Valar, who had been a certified USEASA examiner since 1954. In 1958, he represented USEASA at the U.S. Ski Association's

Whimsical figurines aided the efforts of the children's ski school at Mittersill. Here, Paula Valar encourages her young daughter Christina. *Dorothy Crossley photo.*

convention in Alta, Utah, and urged the group to establish a national ski instruction methodology and certification process. In 1961, he became the founding vice-president and technical committee chair of PSIA, which fifty years later continues to maintain certification standards and provide education for instructors.

"Before that…the American Ski Association was seven divisions, and each division ran their own certification program," Valar said in a 2004 interview. "The idea [behind PSIA] was to protect the customers…from unqualified people."[204] In 1963, Valar literally helped write the book on American skiing, coauthoring *The Official American Ski Technique*, of which he wrote the technical and methodological sections.[205]

As he was leading American skiing and representing PSIA at international meetings of ski professionals, Valar was also working to improve skiing at home in New Hampshire. In addition to the Valars' ski schools, Paul worked in conjunction with the Franconia Ski Club to develop a junior race training program. Each winter from 1959 to 1969, he enticed former members of the Swiss ski team to come to Franconia to instruct during the week and train the ski club's juniors on weekends.

In 1973, the Valars gave up the Cannon ski school but remained directly involved in running Mittersill. Paul was mountain manager there from 1973 to 1979, struggling to maintain a dying ski area without adequate finances. Paula managed Mittersill's hotel and land sales from 1978 to 1979 and became a realtor and rental agent in the area. Paula was also an integral member of the Franconia Notch Chamber of Commerce and the key promoter of the annual weeklong Frostbite Follies Festival held for many years each February in Franconia. "She had that dynamic personality," said Kim Cowles, who bought the Valars' downtown Franconia ski shop from Paul and Paula in 1980 and ran it as the Franconia Sport Shop for more than twenty-five years. "[Paula] was very active in the chamber…in promoting the whole area around Mittersill and Cannon."[206] The Valars were instrumental in the late 1970s in founding and raising funds to open the New England Ski Museum, located adjacent to the Tramway Valley Station at Cannon. Paul was the museum's founding president, from 1977 until 1982, when the museum opened, and he remained on the board until 1989.

After the Valars gave up the Cannon ski school, Jon Putnam, a certified PSIA examiner who had instructed for the Valars, took over the operation for a few years. When Putnam left, a group of his instructors—Phoebe Chardon, Bill Cunningham, Grant Dowse, Gary Harwood and Dick Ogburn—collaborated to run the ski school, hiring veteran instructors and devoted Cannon skiers. Instructor training was a key aspect for the group, and they maintained a connection with Paul Valar, who would occasionally run clinics for the Cannon instructors. "Over the years, we probably had the best skiing staff of any New England ski school," Harwood said. "We spent

Bill Cunningham, Phoebe Chardon, Dick Ogburn and Gary Harwood, who cooperatively ran the ski school at Cannon for many years, beginning in the late 1970s. *Courtesy Gary and Beth Harwood.*

a lot of time on training, but I think importantly, the people that were there loved to ski…We all liked doing what we were doing and being out there."[207]

When the state took over the ski school operation about 1990, Bill Cunningham and his wife, Carol, directed the Cannon Mountain school for a while, and Bill later acted as technical director. The Cunninghams were followed by Mick O'Gara, then Jack McGurin, who was ski school director for a decade, ending his tenure in 2005.[208] Now called the Snowsports School to encompass both skiing and snowboarding, Cannon's learning program in 2011 included nearly one hundred instructors, led by director Irv Fountain.

For their skiing accomplishments and contributions made to American skiing, the Valars were inducted into the U.S. National Ski Hall of Fame—Paula in 1970 and Paul in 1985. The Valars lived their golden years in the chalet they built at the base of Mittersill, on land they purchased from Hubert von Pantz several years after he left Franconia. Paula Valar died in 2001, several months after suffering a major stroke. Paul skied into his eighties and died on Christmas Day 2007. Both of them spent their final days and moments at home in Mittersill, near the runs they had skied for decades, where they had introduced countless others to the joys of the sport and where they had worked, together, to transform American skiing. Through all the sport's changes—in lifts, grooming, equipment, fashion—Paul Valar maintained to the end that the technique, in which he was so very skilled, remained the same: "Skiing is skiing, and it hasn't really changed much."[209]

THE FRANCONIA
SKI CLUB

Leading the Way Downhill

Before the Taft was completed on Cannon Mountain, before the tramway was installed there to carry skiers to the summit, there was the Franconia Ski Club (FSC). Founded in April 1933, the FSC was instrumental in building ski trails in the region, promoting Franconia as a ski center and advocating for the development of Cannon as a ski area. In its earliest years, the ski club hosted events from local and national ski meets to summer softball games and festive dances. Through nearly eight decades, the FSC has evolved into a successful junior race training program, which counts among its past members a dozen inductees to the U.S. National Ski Hall of Fame and several Olympians, including Bode Miller.

Founded by Roland Peabody, Robert Peckett and other prominent residents of the area, the Franconia Ski Club boasted 116 adult members and 26 children at its inception.[210] Many were skiers already, including some accomplished racers, but others were simply local residents interested in using the skiing boom that was sweeping the nation for the betterment of the Franconia area. Eight founding members signed the club's charter on April 21, 1933, establishing the Franconia Ski Club:

> *For the social recreation and improvement of its members, fostering and developing outdoor sports such as skiing, skating, hunting, fishing, building and constructing trails and huts, and such other social and athletic activities as may be for the benefit of its members; to arrange and conduct skiing exhibitions, and matches between its members and other clubs.*[211]

Signatures on the charter include Peabody and innkeeper Edward McKenzie of Franconia; attorney (later judge) Henry Dodge, Kenneth Foley, John Mathes and dentist Stephen Eaton of Littleton; and Stephen Simonds and Hascall Stimson of Lisbon.[212] The club's inaugural officers were Peabody as president, McKenzie as vice-president, Dodge as secretary, Franconia postmaster Arthur Sawyer as treasurer and Robert Peckett as honorary chairman. Other members of the club's first board of directors were Kate Peckett, Lucie Bowles and Leo Hibbard.[213]

Ski club members gathered that spring of 1933 for the all-day jovial affairs typical of ski races of the era. In March, according to a newspaper clipping in the Enzo Serafini Collection, some one hundred club members congregated at Edward McKenzie's Spooner Farm on the Easton Road in Franconia (where the Franconia Inn is now located) for dinner following a race on the first completed section of the Taft Trail. There, they discussed

FSC boys from Dow Academy at the base of the Kinsman Trail near the Franconia-Easton town line, circa 1930s. Racing was an all-day affair then; notice the cookstove and soup pot in the background. *From left*: Whitney Brooks, Bertram Herbert, Raymond Bowles and Norwood Ball. *Charles Trask photo, NESM Collection.*

developing ski trails, fishing grounds and bridle paths, and "the fostering of a spirit of hospitality to all who come within our gates for the enjoyment of sports." Another clip from the same collection reveals that in early April 1933, more than one hundred club members and guests gathered a bit farther out in the Easton Valley at Lucie Bowles's Pleasant View Farm (now Kinsman Lodge), at the base of the Kinsman Trail, for cross-country, slalom and downhill races for adults and juniors, making "the hillsides…gay with the bright colorings of the winter sports costumes." The races were followed by a "maple sugar supper…[and] an old-time 'sing.'"

During the summer of 1933, the club hosted dances to raise funds for building and maintaining ski trails. The FSC hired former Dartmouth and Olympic skier Charley Proctor to inspect local trails and make recommendations for their improvement and for clearing new trails. At the same time, the state's Ski Trails Committee was working with the CCC to develop trails, and the Taft was being completed by the CCC after construction had begun the previous summer, thanks largely to Kate Peckett's efforts.

The timing of the club's founding corresponded closely with Alexander Bright's proposal to build an aerial tramway at Cannon Mountain, and in April 1934, Franconia Ski Club members urged the state to pursue the tramway project, noting that skiing had provided some $30,000 in revenue to Franconia the previous winter.[214] During the country's first winter sports exposition in Boston in December 1935, club members Sig Buchmayr, Roland Peabody and others presented a Franconia Ski Club exhibit, complete with a map of Franconia-area ski trails.[215] In 1936, four of FSC's junior members—Norwood Ball, Bertram Herbert, Roger Peabody and Bobby Clark—traveled to Madison Square Garden in New York City for the winter sports show there. Under Buchmayr's direction and on an indoor, man-made slope covered in crushed ice, the teenagers conducted a skiing demonstration for some twelve thousand winter sports enthusiasts each day of the weeklong show.[216]

The ski club continued in its role of public relations vehicle for the region for decades. As part of its annual agreement with the New Hampshire Division of Parks during the 1950s and '60s, the FSC agreed to "work closely with [the] park manager in establishing major races that could achieve widespread publicity."[217] Led by the duo of Jack Kenney, witty innkeeper of Tamarack, and Enzo Serafini, a local innkeeper and journalist who served for many years as editor of the *Eastern Ski Bulletin* and is a member of the U.S. National Ski Hall of Fame, the club placed regular and copious articles in the local newspaper, as well as in Boston and New York publications during the 1940s and '50s.

Throughout its early decades, the FSC stepped beyond skiing and organized social activities to ensure that both visitors and locals had plenty to do around town. The club maintained the ice-skating rink in town, ran a ski tow at Forest Hills, constructed a ski jump on Fox Hill and sponsored a holiday decorating contest to "brighten...the town up and [let] people know what exists as they drive through the night."[218] For many years, the FSC hosted more Saturday night dances—complete with orchestras—than ski races during winter months. One dance in 1947, titled the "Gay Nineties Party," was held in February at the Franconia Town Hall with waltzes, fox trots and "round and square dances." Admission was sixty cents, and costumes were encouraged, with movie star and part-time Sugar Hill resident Bette Davis acting as a costume judge.[219]

The FSC also organized lodging and dinners for out-of-town racers during ski competitions. In 1939, "approximately forty-five housewives... expressed their willingness to cooperate with the Club at the time of ski meets by furnishing participants their board and lodgings." Luckily for the housewives, someone also suggested organizing suppers at the town hall for racers.[220]

The club remained active year round, with bowling parties, cookouts and swimming outings to Echo Lake in Franconia Notch and Forest Lake in Whitefield during summer months.[221] In the 1940s, Roger Peabody organized an immensely popular summer softball league through the FSC. The games, held at the Dow Academy field, were the cause of both serious competition and much merriment and often resulted in broken windows at the school. "All the kids were up there on their bikes running around, and the guys were all drinking beer," remembers Joan Hannah, whose mother, Paulie, was an ace pitcher in the league, as well as a devoted fundraiser for the FSC and USEASA for many years.[222]

Some of the funds raised through dances and other efforts—Monte Carlo nights with casino games and auctions, or the Road-E-O car races on Echo Lake or on an iced-over field at Lovett's—were used to pay race entry fees for FSC members. In 1947, the club allocated $150 to assist Peg Taylor Kenney and Sel Hannah in their efforts at the Olympic team trials. While neither earned the chance to compete in the 1948 Olympics, their participation in the trials shows that the FSC had a presence at the national ski racing level. Kenney narrowly missed a berth on the Olympic team. Hannah, who had been named to the U.S. Nordic team for the 1940 Olympics, when the

Vintage cars race on Echo Lake during the Road-E-O, held to raise funds for the FSC during the 1950s. *Charles Trask photo, NESM Collection.*

Games were cancelled due to World War II, also missed out. He returned the funds to the club, along with a letter of thanks, saying he "was in the events primarily for the fun of it."[223]

Fun has been a big part of the ski club since its inception and was evident during the first FSC President's Cup relay race in 1955. The race was held for several years and consisted of four legs: the first from the top of Taft Slalom and up the saddle to the top of the Tucker Brook Trail, the second through the thirteen turns of Tucker Brook to the flats, the third across the flats and the fourth to the finish line at the Horse & Hound Inn.

During the inaugural President's Cup, the winning team took advantage of somewhat vague rules and mounted its fourth racer onto a pony named Billy. This twist resulted in "a breathtaking contest between David Symmes, the #4 member of the C team and Gloria Chadwick, the #4 member of the D team mounted, for the first time in her life, on pony Billy, the property of Jym Dudley, the D team captain."[224] Billy's participation was all in good fun, but the announcement for subsequent President's Cup races noted that all participants should be "human bipeds" and stipulated in bold print, "No ponies!"[225] A skillful racer—with or without a pony—Chadwick in later years

102

would manage U.S. Olympic and FIS teams, serve as executive secretary for the United States Ski Association and direct the U.S. Olympic Training Center in Marquette, Michigan. She was inducted into the U.S. National Ski Hall of Fame in 1986.[226]

Among the regular and more serious FSC-sponsored races in the 1950s and '60s was the club's annual preseason meet in December—if there was enough snow—which consisted of giant slalom (GS), slalom, cross country and jumping events and included many college competitors. During the late 1950s, the winner of the giant slalom event earned the Joel S. Coffin III Memorial Bowl, in honor of Robert Peckett's grandson, a member of the fabled 10th Mountain Division who was killed in action during World War II in Iola, Italy.[227] The trophy had previously been awarded to the combined winner of the annual Hochgebirge race and was originally retired by Brooks Dodge in 1954, after he won the bowl three consecutive years. The club also helped run the Cannon races, held regularly until the mid-1960s, where competitors would race the clock from summit to base on the Cannon Trail

Joel Coffin in the snow fields at Cannon's summit. He is wearing the uniform designed by Saks Fifth Avenue for the 1936 Winter Sports Show at Madison Square Garden, where he and a group of FSC boys demonstrated skiing. *Charles Trask photo, NESM Collection.*

in an attempt to earn a "Gold Cannon" and the bragging rights associated with such a feat.

In 1956, the FSC hosted the Junior National Championships at Cannon Mountain. This was the first time all four events of the Juniors—cross-country, jumping, downhill and slalom—were held in the East. The club raised some $5,000 to prepare for the event, which included construction of a forty-meter ski jump just south of the tramway's Valley Station.

FSC juniors Joan Hannah, Bruce Leavitt and Gordi Eaton competed in the Junior Nationals at Cannon. Hannah, for whom the 1956 competition was the third of four Junior Nationals in which she would race, won the downhill and finished tenth in the slalom to earn a third-place finish in the combined. Eaton, whose father signed the FSC charter in 1933, was thirty-fifth in the slalom, and a third-place downhill finish moved him into the fifteenth spot in the combined.[228] Both racers, then sixteen years old, would race in the Olympics four years later.

Hannah and Eaton found ski racing success before the FSC had any semblance of modern junior race training programs. Their training consisted of school-run ski outings and weeklong training sessions during the winter break from classes. Ollie Cole, who had moved to Franconia

FSC racer Joan Hannah competes at Cannon during the 1956 Junior Nationals. *Courtesy Joan Hannah.*

after World War II to teach at Dow Academy and in Paul Valar's ski school, helped organize the junior program during the 1950s.[229] Cole and the FSC introduced area youngsters to skiing, providing instruction and equipment to anyone interested, in large part through the Roland Peabody Memorial Fund, established by the FSC after Peabody's death. The ski club regularly placed junior racers on Eastern Junior National teams, and three FSC juniors traveled to Whitefish, Montana, for the 1955 Junior Nationals. The club provided financial help to racers for the long trip west and paid the way for Cole, who accompanied the juniors as a coach for the eastern contingent.[230]

In the winter of 1959–60, with the assistance of Paul Valar, the FSC began importing Swiss ski racers—Roland Blaesi, Paul Pfosi and Hans Jaeger among them—to coach the club's juniors on weekends and teach ski lessons for his ski schools during the week. During the 1960s, the U.S. Eastern Amateur Ski Association mandated full membership in USEASA for clubs who wished to hold sanctioned races or sponsor racers in competitions, and the ski club was necessarily reorganized, shifting its focus primarily to junior race training. Former FSC racer Dave Boyle was hired as the club's first full-time coach in 1969, beginning a long tradition of Franconia Ski Club racers returning to the club's roster as coaches.

As the club's purpose and activities evolved, so did its membership, gradually moving from almost entirely local residents to include several families from out of town and out of state. In 1970, the FSC listed seventy-five junior racers, including fifty-three from New Hampshire and twenty-two from other states.[231] Training headquarters was the tiny timing shack at the bottom of the Banshee Trail. In 1976, the club happily moved into new headquarters at the base of Gary's Trail. Christened Ernie's Haus, the building was given to the state by the Glaessel family in memory of their son, Ernst Jr., who died while serving in the navy in 1973. Although he wasn't a racer, Ernie loved skiing and loved Cannon Mountain, where he had learned the sport from Marge and Mickey Libby.[232]

Marge and Mickey were friends to countless youngsters who learned to ski at Cannon. They quietly looked after many Cannon kids, volunteering at the annual Peabody and Whitcomb memorial races, transporting children to competitions, making sure any child interested in skiing had the proper equipment to enjoy the sport and teaching youngsters to ski. Among the young skiers the Libbys helped nurture was Bode Miller, Jack and Peg Kenney's grandson, who grew up as a neighbor to the Libbys in Easton, was an FSC junior during the 1980s, and went on to become the most successful

American ski racer in history. Many others learned the sport and garnered encouragement from Marge and Mickey.

In 2011, the ski club boasted more than 140 junior racers from ages eight to eighteen, plus about fifty racers from the Holderness School, which trains in collaboration with the FSC. The majority of these racers are from southern New Hampshire or other New England states, but a couple dozen local children also race for the club. A staff of nearly twenty coaches—more than half of them former FSC racers—oversees the race training for these youngsters, and ski club families continue to volunteer countless hours throughout the winter to run races and organize related club activities.[233] The club's main fundraisers now include a live and silent auction held annually in February and a fall golf tournament, dubbed the "Nines of the Notch."

Included in the various junior competitions the FSC holds each winter are events commemorating local skiers. The Peter Kenney Memorial Slalom is held in January in honor of one of the Kenneys' sons, who died in 1981 when his kayak capsized on Echo Lake. The Dowse Memorial in February honors Grant and Pegge Dowse, founders of the Garnet Hill company in Franconia and FSC boosters, who died in a 1985 plane crash. The Pendoley Memorial Slalom is held each March in memory of Cannon ski shop employee and FSC supporter Mark Pendoley, who died in 1985 on Cannon's Rocket Trail.[234] In 1979, the FSC established the Ross Coffin Memorial Scholarship, honoring the brother of Joel S. Coffin III and grandson of Robert Peckett. Ross Coffin was a devoted supporter of the club and traveled at his own expense with FSC juniors in the 1950s when they competed in races around the country.

The club remains directly involved in running the annual Roland Peabody and Gary Whitcomb memorial races for local schoolchildren in February, as well as a number of local high school competitions. Every two or three years, the FSC plays host to the top ten male and female high school skiers from each state from as far west as Wisconsin and as far south as Virginia during the Eastern High School Championships.[235] The FSC also collaborates with the Ski Club Hochgebirge to host the annual Hochgebirge Challenge Cup.

Among the club's proudest accomplishments in recent years is the development of a giant slalom racecourse, running from Middle Ravine onto Turnpike. In 2011, the club began planning for the future creation of a training and racing venue for the speed events of Super-G and downhill, something Cannon has not seen since the 1967 World Cup races. The options under consideration for such a trail include reviving and adding snowmaking to the Baron's Run on Mittersill, which includes a section of the historic Taft Race Trail, and reworking C-93, the downhill course for

Standing in front of club headquarters, Ernie's Haus at Cannon, FSC alumni coaching for the club in 2011 included, from left, Trevor Hamilton, Steve Roberts, Erin Fletcher, Nathan Lovett, Jody Lozeau, Ryan Boissonneault, Cory Mckim, and Allyson Newell. *Author photo.*

the 1967 World Cup. "We've got pretty exciting plans for our future," said FSC Program Director Trevor Hamilton, who grew up racing in the club and has been a coach there since 1998. "Sometimes having a history creates a history, or creates a future…There's a very proud history affiliated with our program."[236]

The majority of Franconia Ski Club members, past and present, are simply people who love the sport and children who are discovering the thrill of racing downhill on skis. Many of these youngsters earn bibs at regional and national championship events each year. Some go on to achieve even greater skiing accomplishments, whether racing in college or for the U.S. Ski Team or joining the growing extreme skiing movement. More importantly, these young skiers develop what the Franconia Ski Club's founders deemed essential nearly eighty years ago: a lifelong passion for the sport of skiing.

THE 1967 WORLD CUP

The World Comes to Cannon

There is one week in Cannon's ski history that stands out from the rest, a week of fierce competition and serious revelry, when the world's biggest skiing stars came to Franconia. During that week in March 1967, the first World Cup races ever held in North America were contested on the slopes of Cannon Mountain. Racers arrived from Europe, Canada and across the country, and the world's press, ski officials and some twenty thousand spectators tagged along, creating an atmosphere that was both cosmopolitan and celebratory.

Ski racing phenomenon Jean-Claude Killy of France was the star, cruising to victory in the downhill, powering through soft snow and ruts in the giant slalom and eking out a win over American favorite Jimmy Heuga on an icy slalom course to complete a sweep of the Cannon events and clinch skiing's first World Cup title. The young American team had a good showing, claiming two medals in the men's races and several top-ten finishes in the women's events against a dominant French team and veteran racers from Austria and Switzerland. Hosting the World Cup involved thousands of volunteer hours, myriad logistics and the considerable effort of creating a course long enough to meet World Cup regulations on a mountain tiny in comparison to the soaring European Alps.

The World Cup, in which a champion is determined based on points accrued at races throughout the season, was in its inaugural year in 1967, and race organizers at Cannon had no precedent to follow. The winter-long competition was the brainchild of French sports writer Serge Lang, who had hashed out the details the previous spring with United States ski team director Bob Beattie and French ski team director Honoré Bonnet.[237] "These guys were clearly forward thinking. They recognized that to really develop our sport, we needed to have every race count," said Gordi Eaton, who had grown up skiing at Cannon, gone on to compete in the Olympics and was a U.S. Ski Team coach in 1967.[238]

"We thought that the World Cup was going to be very important. I think we felt that it was going to be maybe more important here in the United States than anywhere else," said Beattie in a 2010 interview. "We knew that in a place like Kitzbuhel, [ski racing] was going to always be important. The Hahnenkamm [downhill] we knew was going to be important for Austria. We felt that the World Cup was going to latch on over here in the United States."[239]

Before arriving at Cannon, the world's best skiers had competed in a series of World Cup events in Europe, with two more to follow in Colorado and Wyoming. The prestige of hosting the first World Cup events in North

The dotted lines on this map of Cannon from the 1967 World Cup program indicate the routes for the downhill, GS and slalom races. *Author's collection.*

America was huge, and Cannon gained that honor in part due to a New Hampshire connection with Eaton and Beattie and in part because the Eastern Inter-Club Ski League (EICSL) was willing to take on the considerable task of hosting the world at Cannon. "We wanted to have [races] all over the place...I'm from New Hampshire, and Cannon Mountain was a great spot for me," said Beattie. "There were a lot of people who grew up at Cannon Mountain—Gordi being one of them, and myself, and a lot of others, too. We really wanted to have [the World Cup] at Cannon, and the people at Cannon Mountain wanted it, too."[240]

The Cannon races were held March 10–12 under the label of the North American Alpine Championships, which had previously consisted of racers only from the United States and Canada. The EICSL, active since 1946, had a membership of five thousand skiers from fifty-three clubs, mainly from the greater Boston area. EICSL had the volunteer power and technical know-how to host this event of international import and intrigue and was recommended for the job by Roger Peabody, then head of the United States Eastern Amateur Ski Association, and other ski racing leaders.[241]

Organizing the World Cup races involved extensive collaboration with the State of New Hampshire and Cannon staff, area chambers of commerce, myriad businesses, the Franconia Ski Club, Sno-engineering and others. The details were endless, and the price tag for the races was more than $100,000. Race organizers had to consider everything from crowd control and parking for thousands of cars to transportation and housing for the competitors and the press corps. The state approved an expenditure of nearly $42,000. Television rights for a live broadcast on CBS paid some of the cost. EICSL, with numerous donations of lodging, equipment and manpower, made up the difference.[242]

Orchestrating every detail from lodging and transportation to recruiting course setters and gatekeepers for the event was race chairman Bill Kempton of EICSL. A lifelong avid skier, Kempton loved competition, and he worked tirelessly to ensure that the World Cup races at Cannon were successful. A few years later, Kempton became president of the Franconia Ski Club—the first from outside the Franconia area—and did much to promote and manage the junior race program. He later retired to Franconia, from his home in Massachusetts, and each winter assembled a "rag-tag bunch of old-timers" dubbed "the Diehards" to compete—adeptly—in the weekly Innkeepers Race at Cannon.[243]

Kempton's associates in running the 1967 races were anything but ragtag and included many EICSL officers and other skilled race officials. J. Leland "Doc" Sosman was chief of course for each event, responsible for making

Race officials survey the downhill course during the summer of 1966. *From left*: Bill Kempton, Willy Schaeffler, "Doc" Sosman and Ned McSherry. *NESM Collection.*

sure all aspects of each racecourse—from start to finish, snow conditions to gate spacing—were correct. A radiologist by trade, Sosman was dedicated to ski racing and for years donated incalculable hours to the sport, including training other volunteers in the various aspects of holding a race. Following the Cannon races, Sosman served as chief of race at several World Cup events at nearby Waterville Valley, his home hill, and was a race official at six Olympic Games. He was inducted into the U.S. National Ski Hall of Fame in 1999.[244]

Serving as technical delegate to the Fédération Internationale de Ski (FIS) at Cannon, to help create the downhill course and ensure that the races met the standards of skiing's international governing body, was the venerable Willy Schaeffler. A native of Austria who had taught General George Patton and his army forces to ski following World War II, Schaeffler coached a hugely successful University of Denver Ski Team in the 1950s and '60s and became U.S. ski team director in 1970. He was inducted into the U.S. National Ski Hall of Fame in 1974.[245]

The biggest physical challenge for holding World Cup races on Cannon was creating a downhill course long enough to meet international racing standards. The course, dubbed C-93, began on Vista Way and ran onto By-Pass, around the sharp corner of Paulie's Extension, and down the sheer face of Avalanche. In the summer of 1966, trail workers removed two islands of trees and widened the corners on Vista Way to prepare for the high-speed downhill. By-Pass was widened, using dynamite to blow through the granite ledge, to meet minimum FIS width requirements. The corner into Avalanche was also widened and graded, but it's still a wicked crank of a turn—nearly a right angle—especially at downhill speeds. Finally, Avalanche had to be extended four hundred feet, practically onto Echo Lake, to make the course long enough by FIS standards. Racers started above the Tram's Mountain Station and ended—2,130 vertical feet and a length of 8,388 feet—below on the old Route 18.[246]

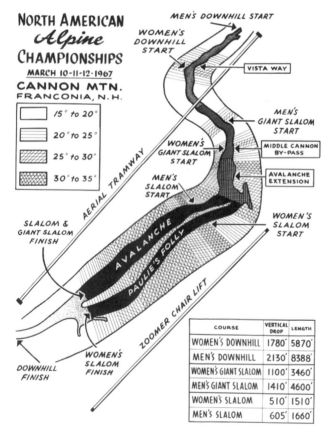

COURSE	VERTICAL DROP	LENGTH
WOMEN'S DOWNHILL	1780'	5870'
MEN'S DOWNHILL	2130'	8388'
WOMEN'S GIANT SLALOM	1100'	3460'
MEN'S GIANT SLALOM	1410'	4600'
WOMEN'S SLALOM	510'	1510'
MEN'S SLALOM	605'	1660'

The course specifications, as outlined in the program for the 1967 World Cup races at Cannon. *Author's collection.*

Laying out the course was just the start of preparations. Some six thousand feet of communications cables were run the length of the downhill course to allow for radio and television broadcasts of the races. Six platforms for the television cameras were erected along the course, with one more at the finish. Workers installed more than twenty-five hundred feet of snow fence, moved 130 bales of hay and strung some five thousand feet of rope for crowd control. Construction companies from around the state donated trailers to be used as first aid stations and waxing rooms for racers. Wildcat Mountain provided snowmobiles for transporting CBS equipment and personnel. The employee lounge in the basement of the Tramway Valley Station was transformed into a crowded pressroom, with twenty-five typewriters on loan from a Manchester company. Tramcar conductors, between trips up and down the mountain, tied flags onto more than three hundred gates needed for the races.[247]

Dozens of EICSL members took a week or more off from their jobs and regular lives to prepare for and work through the World Cup races, handling everything from foot packing the courses to serving as timers and gatekeepers. "I can't tell you the hours that those guys spent putting this thing together," said Eaton. "It turned out to be just a booming success…Those ski clubs did a bang-up job."[248] Locally based Sno-engineering shut down for two weeks leading to the races so its small but vastly knowledgeable crew could help prepare the mountain for the arrival of the world's best skiers. At that time, Sno-engineering included Sel Hannah, Joe Cushing, Ted Farwell and Jim Branch, who collectively possessed several decades of experience in ski racing, trail design and ski area management.

Race preparations were complicated by the lack of snow at Cannon in early March. With no snowmaking system until 1969, Cannon was still entirely reliant on natural snow during the World Cup races. Any other year, the mountain could have simply closed trails or shut down altogether—but not in 1967, with the world watching. With the World Cup quickly approaching and the snow pack at Cannon dwindling, mountain workers and EICSL volunteers got to work moving snow from wherever they could find it onto the racecourse. Ski patrolman Rich Millen, who also coached the neighboring Littleton High School football team, recruited a dozen teenagers to haul snow out of the woods and onto the trail. "We'd go in the woods…throw the snow onto chutes and bring it out on the trails," Millen recalled. "We did that for about five days. Then all of a sudden we got dumped with about a twenty-inch storm."[249]

The snow haulers quickly shifted gears, becoming snow packers. Millen's student helpers joined more than one hundred EICSL volunteers to sidestep the entire course. Meanwhile, a week before the downhill, the state had enlisted Charles Skinner of Grand Rapids, Minnesota, to haul his portable snowmaking system halfway across the country and set up shop on Avalanche.[250] A crew of a few dozen workers assisted Skinner, using portable compressors and fire hoses to pump water from Echo Lake as high up Avalanche as the hose would reach.[251]

The racers arrived early in the week and were hosted by area inns, which donated lodging and board for all the foreign teams. The Austrians, of course, were at Mittersill. The Swiss lodged at Raynor's Motel and ate at the Village House in Franconia. The French stayed at Lovett's Inn in Franconia, the Germans at Wayside Inn in Bethlehem, the Canadians at Continental 93 in Littleton and the Italians at the Horse & Hound Inn in Franconia. American racers were put up by area residents during the week of training and competition.[252]

Following three days of downhill training, racing began Friday amid spring-like conditions. Killy and teammate Guy Perrillat took the top two spots in the downhill, with Killy nearly a second ahead of the rest of the field. Jim Barrows, a twenty-two-year-old American skier, claimed third place—to the delight of the mostly American crowd of spectators. The following year, during the Olympics in Grenoble, Barrows took an incredible crash that famously appeared on ABC's *Wide World of Sports* and ended his bid for Olympic gold and his season. French skiers Isabelle Mir and Annie Famose and Austrian Erika Schineggor led the women's field in the downhill, where Suzy Chaffee, in tenth place, was the top American finisher.

Saturday's giant slalom, running from By-Pass down Avalanche, was contested on "a rut-strewn ice slide" as temperatures rose to nearly fifty degrees. The Austrian team celebrated briefly when a five-second timing error put Herbert Huber in the lead, but the mistake was quickly remedied, and Huber was relegated to ninth place. Killy "forced his will upon the mountain" to claim his second victory in as many days, as the French team dominated once again, claiming the top two spots in both the men's and women's competitions. The giant slalom win also clinched the World Cup crown for Killy, who won twelve of eighteen World Cup races that first season and remains one of the winningest ski racers in history. Canada's Nancy Greene, who would go on to claim the women's World Cup title two weeks later, took third place in the GS at Cannon.[253]

Race volunteers put in more hard time on Saturday afternoon, packing the sun-softened snow on Avalanche and Paulie's to prepare for Sunday's slalom races. "That night [the temperature] went down to about zero," said Sno-engineering's Joe Cushing in an interview on May 10, 2010. "And the

Jean-Claude Killy cruises to victory in the giant slalom on Avalanche. *Dorothy Crossley photo.*

course was absolutely perfect. [The racers] loved it…It was sort of side-stepped ice. Of course, number 50 still had a good course to race."

Some of the racers may have loved the hardened course, but it proved too much to handle for many. More than half the women's field—twenty-two of thirty-nine racers—failed to complete two runs on Paulie's Folly. While the French women claimed the top three spots, the Americans placed six racers in the top ten. The men's slalom on Avalanche was a nail-biter. American Jimmy Heuga dissected the second run course with quick precision to earn the fastest time of the run, but Killy's speedier first run earned him his third victory of the weekend by seven-hundredths of a second. Austria's Huber took third place to earn some glory after the previous day's disappointment.

There was a hometown contingent, as well, although it didn't include any race favorites. Gordi Eaton and Paul Valar both served as course setters. Joan Hannah, who had retired from the national team the previous winter, foreran all three women's events. Another former Franconia Ski Club racer, Bill Kenney, foreran the men's downhill, and some of the FSC's top juniors served as unofficial forerunners on the downhill course. FSC alumnus and U.S. Ski Team member Duncan Cullman placed thirty-eighth in a field of fifty-five in the downhill. Fred Libby, son of Marge and Mickey, and Dave Boyle, both past members of the FSC, also competed. Libby finished twenty-second in the men's GS and fifty-first in the downhill, and Boyle was twenty-sixth in the GS and fifty-fourth in the downhill.[254]

In an era of stopwatch timing, the World Cup races at Cannon were the first in the East to use computer scoring. An IBM computer calculated up-to-the-minute results, displayed the times of the top ten competitors on a scoreboard during the races, processed final results and updated each racer's accumulated World Cup points at the races.[255] (The timing blunder in the men's GS was attributed to human error.)

The World Cup spectacle drew upwards of twenty thousand spectators to the Notch during the weekend. Cannon skiers, enthusiasts of the sport and curious onlookers lined the slopes. Some even climbed trees alongside the trail to gain a better view.[256] "There were an awful lot of old-time skiers who came. Anybody who had ever skied Cannon…They just had to come and see this," said Dick Hamilton, longtime promoter of the White Mountains and then head of the Ski 93 organization. "It was wonderful, really. Never has Cannon seen so many people and so many admirers. It was probably Cannon's greatest day."[257]

Those fans who weren't crowded on the hill to watch the races gathered in the lounge at Mittersill or other local watering holes to watch Sunday's races live on the CBS *Sports Spectacular*, cheering wildly for the Americans. With many thousands of extra people, from volunteers and spectators to racers and ski officials, crammed into the small-town inns, bars and ski slopes around

A huge crowd gathered to watch the World Cup races at Cannon. *Dorothy Crossley photo.*

Franconia, a festive atmosphere settled over the town the week of the World Cup races. "At night…you could hardly go anywhere without running into a party, gargantuan in size or relatively small," wrote Ralph "Deak" Morse of the State Division of Economic Development following the event. "It was Mardi Gras, New Year's Eve, Bastille Day, carnival and carousel all wrapped into one. It was wonderbar and fantastique and glorious in whatever tongue you chose to say it."[258]

News from the World Cup was relayed around the world by a press corps of more than two hundred, including the CBS television crew, radio broadcasters and print reporters representing everything from the smallest local papers to major magazines and international publications. Writers from all the ski magazines were there, along with reporters from the *Washington Post* and the *New York Times*, the *Christian Science Monitor*, *Sports Illustrated* and myriad international publications, including *L'Equipe*, represented by Serge Lang. In the tiny pressroom, Killy once climbed atop a table with his translator so reporters could see him and hear his responses to their endless questions.[259]

The World Cup moved west from Cannon to Vail, Colorado, which continues to host World Cup races annually, and Jackson Hole, Wyoming, to close out the 1967 season. Cannon has never hosted another downhill event or World Cup race, although nearby Waterville Valley, which was opened by Olympian Tom Corcoran just prior to the 1967 races at Cannon, has put on eleven World Cup events (but no downhills), including the World Cup Finals in 1969 and 1991.[260] "What it eventually took was a ski area that decides, this is how we want to spend our dollars," said Gordi Eaton. "When it came time to decide where these World Cups were going to be held, Tommy [Corcoran] was right there in the front row saying, 'They're going to be held at Waterville.' That's what it took… Cannon, being state run, there was not a single person that had that control."[261]

FIS rules also changed to require a vertical drop of eight hundred meters—about 2,625 feet—for a downhill course. Cannon's claim to the longest vertical of any New Hampshire ski area is still far short of that, at 2,180 feet. And so the world moved on to bigger mountains, and Cannon faded back into what it had been before that week in March 1967: a quiet ski area carved from forests and New Hampshire granite by some of American skiing's best characters and run by the state. But for those who were there during the few days the world came to Cannon, and for all the skiers who have found their groove to arc a perfect turn from Paulie's Extension onto Avalanche or schussed Avalanche in a tuck and a thrilling rush of adrenaline, the spirit of America's first World Cup ski races lingers on Cannon Mountain.

CANNON TRAILS AND THEIR STORIES

The trails at Cannon are a map to the mountain's ski history. The earliest ski runs, cut when the tramway was still a novelty, wind down from the summit, falling like tendrils toward the valley floor. The lakeside runs developed in the 1950s and 1960s are wider, built for speed, turned like a handful of fingers toward the tramway's Valley Station. The Cannonball Trail built in 1990 cuts a wide, straight swath down the upper third of the mountain, screaming for attention amidst its more humble neighbors. The newest trails, at the base of the mountain, are quiet and gentle, reaching toward Mittersill and the reunion with that area. The trail names speak of the mountain's stories: Taft, Gary's, Paulie's Folly, Hardscrabble, Spookie, Gremlin and Jasper's Hideaway. There are also names that don't appear on any map (Mickey's Corner, Rock Garden, Gun Sight, Saddle Sore) and those that have disappeared from the map with the passing of time (Shirley's Slope and Asa's Acre). On a mountain with many tales to tell, the trails shed light on a few of Cannon's stories.

When the Cannon Mountain Aerial Tramway opened in 1938, there were few runs to choose from: Taft Slalom, Taft Racecourse, Cannon, Coppermine and Tucker Brook. Of those, only the Taft Slalom and Cannon Trails were actually on Cannon Mountain, with the others accessible via a hike from the bottom of Taft Slalom over the saddle to Mount Jackson (later the Mittersill ski area). Skiers staying on Cannon could link to the Fleitman Trail, a cross-country-style trail bringing skiers eventually back to the Valley Station. These early trails were winding and narrow, designed to

This circa 1940 view shows the Cannon and Ravine Trails on Cannon Mountain and the Taft Race Trail winding down Mount Jackson. *Charles Trask photo, NESM Collection.*

hold whatever natural snow fell in the days before snowmaking systems and grooming machines. They were cut so they would not be visible from the highway through the Notch, a condition of the Forest Society's blessing to building the tramway at Cannon. Gradually, the trails were widened, some were straightened, and many more were added. Cannon's trail map for the 2010–11 ski season listed seventy-two named trails.

Building any trail on Cannon, let alone seventy-two of them, was a challenge from the start. The first trail there—the famous Taft—took two summers and a crew of Civilian Conservation Corps men to complete. The others were developed after the tramway opened, transforming Cannon from a mountain with a ski trail into a bona fide ski area. Of all the hundreds of ski areas Sel Hannah helped create, he claimed Cannon was the most difficult to shape. "It's been a real stinker to work on," he said during a 1979 interview. "[It's] all ledge and…either too steep or too flat or too rocky…It's the windiest mountain I guess that anyone has ever tried to develop."[262] One of the first areas of the mountain Hannah worked on was the middle section of the original Cannon Trail—known now as Middle Cannon. It's an area particularly prone to Cannon's famous winds, which have scoured snow from the stony ledge of that section since the trail's earliest days, earning the spot where Middle Cannon becomes Lower Cannon the nickname of Rock Garden.

Early trail crews did not enjoy the luxuries of bulldozers or chainsaws to aid them as they reshaped the mountain. They had only axes, crowbars and brute strength as tools. Groups of men worked systematically, following the string that "sidelined" the outer edges of the trail. First the "axe men" cut and limbed large trees along the trail. The workers who followed piled the brush to be burned and sawed the downed trees into manageable lengths. Another pair removed stumps with grub axes, while two more men used crowbars to pry protruding rocks from the ground. A second crew followed the first, using dynamite to remove larger rocks—although at Cannon, use of explosives was limited for fear of damaging the Old Man of the Mountain.[263]

By necessity, the early trails were narrow and cleared of as many rocks, roots and stumps as possible. Without the benefit—or even the thought—of snowmaking, the trails needed to be skiable on as little as a few inches of snow. Narrower trails provided protection from the wind and, of course, required less effort to construct and maintain. Most trails were not wider

This map shows the trail system circa 1960. Note the three T-bars linking the base to the summit on Cannon; only Gary's, Zoomer and Paulie's (#3, 2, 1) cut lakeside; the Taft Race Trail (#14) is still marked; and Route 18 runs along the west side of Echo Lake. *NESM Collection.*

than fifty feet, and many were much narrower, in some places tapering to as little as fifteen feet wide. "We used to kid about it when we were racing sometimes and say that you could touch your elbows on the trees," said Roger Peabody.[264]

Grooming was another early challenge. When Cannon opened, Roland Peabody employed a crew of snow shovelers who would fill in ruts along the trail. Ski patrollers followed to sidestep and pack the snow. Gradually, rudimentary snow rollers, then snow cats, were introduced, and grooming equipment evolved. Today's grooming machines chop through the most boilerplate of ice, smoothing snow into neat rows of "corduroy."

While many of Cannon's trail names are simply situational—Cannon named for the mountain, Ravine because it was cut along a natural gully and Vista Way for its stellar view of Mount Lafayette and Franconia Notch—others have meaning that may not be ascertained from a simple reading of the trail map. Hardscrabble, one of Cannon's earliest trails, for instance, was named for Hardscrabble Hill, what most folks today know as Three Mile Hill, Route 18 from town to the mountain.[265]

Early skiers named landmarks along trails for people and events. The Taft Race Trail included Bright's Corner, where Alec Bright once careened off the course, and Constant's Tree, where a young army captain named Victor Constant was killed during a training run at the 1946 U.S. Nationals.[266] That naming tradition has continued at Cannon with such landmarks as Mickey's Corner. Although you won't find that name on any official trail map (there is a Mickey's Margin at Cannon, but it's in an entirely different area of the mountain), any ski patroller knows where it is: the last turn at the bottom of Upper Ravine, where it meets the Skylight trail.

Mickey Libby was a ski patroller at Cannon for more than forty years. He grew up in Berlin and after serving in the army during World War II moved to Franconia to work as a ski instructor for Benno Rybizka at Mittersill. He married local girl Marge Herbert and in the late 1940s started working on the Cannon Ski Patrol, retiring as patrol director in 1989. "Mickey Libby was just a beautiful, artistic skier. He was sort of the representative for the mountain," said Jere Peabody. "He spent more time out skiing with the people and drumming them up to love Cannon. He was just like an ambassador when he was on the patrol."[267]

Despite his artistry, however, like any skier, Mickey also took a few falls. The worst came during an afternoon sweep of the trails, when Mickey went hard into the woods at the bottom of Upper Ravine. He ended up suspended upside-down in the trees, with two busted-up knees and a broken back. It

Mickey Libby on Cannon Mountain. *Courtesy Bill Mead.*

took seven months in bed to heal. Ever since that crash, the last turn on the trail has been known as Mickey's Corner. "It's not much of a corner but it's a change of light as well as direction," Mickey remembered years later. "I took a lot of [crashes] but…I don't remember them like that one."[268]

Other runs at Cannon are officially named for people. The Taft, of course, was named for Richard Taft, proprietor of the grand Profile House in the 1800s. Gary's trail was originally called Benson's, named for the logger who helped clear the trail. It has long been called Gary's, after Gary Whitcomb, a ski patroller at Cannon who died in an automobile accident as a young man.[269] There used to be a Shirley's Slope, by the old Banshee T-bar, named after Roland Peabody's secretary Shirley Johnson.[270] A short spur linking the tramway to By-Pass is dubbed David's Detour for longtime ski patroller David Harris, who died of cancer in the 1990s.[271]

The pony slope, recently renamed Huckerbrook, was for years called Asa's Acre. Asa was the nickname of Bob Finn, who worked at Cannon for more than three decades, beginning in the late 1940s. He started on ski patrol and then worked many years as a tramcar conductor. During the summers, Finn was the resident sign maker in Franconia Notch, carving by hand the wooden signs that marked everything from ski trails to highway exits. His shop was in the Peabody building, looking out over the pony slope, which subsequently became Asa's Acre.[272]

Cannon's most precipitous trail—D.J.'s Tramline—opened in 2003, tumbling over the boulders along the steep drop underneath the tramway. The trail, originally called simply Tramline, was renamed in 2009 for one of the Cannon ski patrollers and trail workers who helped clear it, a young man loved by many in and around Franconia Notch. D.J. Stelmat was killed in 2008, at the age of twenty-seven, while serving as an army medic in the Iraq war.

Paulie's Folly, built in 1950 and now tucked between the Zoomer and Avalanche Trails, is named for Paulie Hannah. Although not as widely famous as her husband, Sel, the trail designer, and daughter Joanie, the Olympian, Paulie Hannah did much to help skiing and local skiers. She was a superb fundraiser, helping to procure $47,000 in donations for the Olympic Committee in 1964[273] (the second of two Olympics in which Joan competed) and ably managing—indeed, helping to establish—the Roland

Paulie Hannah races at Reno, Nevada, in the 1940s. *Courtesy Joan Hannah.*

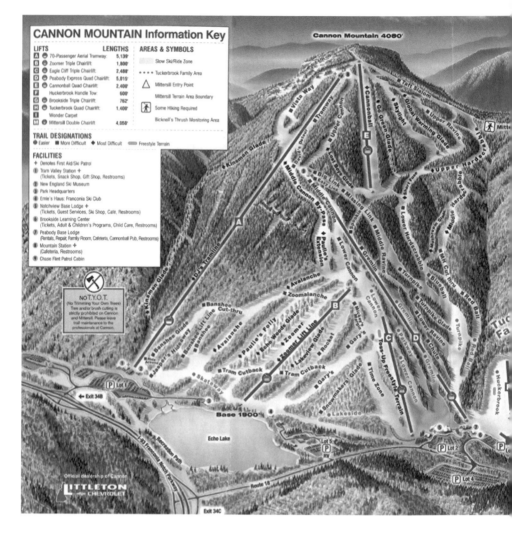

Peabody Memorial Fund in its earliest years. She also kept the books for Sel's Sno-engineering and managed the family's Ski Hearth Farm.

Paulie Hannah did all of that from the confines of a wheelchair. In 1949, at age thirty-two, Paulie contracted polio and was almost completely paralyzed for the rest of her long life. Only months before, the mother of four young children had cruised to victory in the first Eastern Giant Slalom Championships, held on the Taft. With polio, she lost her ability to ski, dance, heft one-hundred-pound bags of potatoes at the farm and create the sculptures she loved to make. But she adopted a motto of "adaptability is everything." With slings attached to her wheelchair to hold her arms partly aloft, Paulie could type with two fingers, scratch out bills for vegetables and

Cannon Mountain's 2010–11 trail map, showing all seventy-two named trails and the Mittersill Terrain Area.

draw the personalized Christmas cards she made each year. "She was tough, tougher than nails," Joan Hannah said of her mother. "She just kept on doing what she could do."[274]

The trail that bears her name is, like Paulie Hannah, both tough and fun. It is steep, almost concave, built to hold snow. It's one of Cannon's quieter trails now, as skiers opt for the wider and straighter runs on either side. But it has seen its share of excitement as the site of serious ski competitions, including the women's slalom during the 1967 World Cup. For a while in the 1960s, when suspenders were the common companion to the first generation of stretch pants, those who skied Paulie's in the light of a full moon earned red suspenders.[275]

People aren't the only ones commemorated in Cannon's trail names. A litter of trails is named after some of the feline characters who have been companions to mountain employees over the years. From the opening of the tramway until the early twenty-first century, there were night watchmen at the Valley Station, and many kept cats for company. The tabby tradition continues at the park headquarters building nearby, where Jasper roams freely, sometimes even joining meetings of legislative bigwigs in the conference room. Among the kitties remembered with trail names are Spookie, Gremlin, Jasper (Jasper's Hideaway) and Banshee.[276]

Other animals appear on the Cannon trail map, too. The Tuckerbrook area, opened in 2003, includes several runs named after critters trail workers spotted while building the trails: Rabbit Path, Turkey Trot, Moose Alley, Deer Run, Bear Paw, Coyote Crossing, Fox Tail and Raven's Ridge. In recent years, Cannon has also added a number of glades to its repertoire. These range from the gentle Robin's Nest Glade in the Tuckerbrook area to the more challenging Lakeview Glade and the gnarly Kinsman Glade.

While Cannon listed seventy-two trails on its 2010–11 map, there are others—secret stashes, if you will—that are unlisted and well hidden but familiar to many Cannon skiers. Tucker Brook, cut during the 1930s by the CCC and long since relinquished to the forest, is perhaps the most well known, but it's still obscured from the eyes of the uninitiated. Its thirteen turns descend from Mount Jackson through hardwood forest to the valley floor a couple of miles from Cannon's Peabody base area. Other more secret spurs like Locals Only branch off Tucker Brook.

A slew of trails bearing names like Saddle Sore, Pony Express, Mardi Gras and Obvious Glade have been clandestinely pared from the forests on and around Cannon by skiers intimate with the local landscape. On the opposite edge of the mountain from those runs over the saddle, South Bowl and Gun Sight—named because of its proximity to the rock formation of a cannon that gave the mountain its name—bring adventurous skiers through the snowfields and down the southern side of the mountain, ending south of the Valley Station. There are more trails over the backside of Cannon, down the Cannonballs.

Cannon skiers all have their preferred runs, whether quick cruisers on the lakeside trails, mountain runs from summit to base along the curvier trails, or seeking out the hidden stashes of untracked powder off the beaten path. For many, the older runs are the favorites, trails like Upper Cannon and Ravine. There, a skier can cling to the contour of the slope, turning with the trail around clusters of frost-stunted spruce trees, dipping down steep inclines, following in the tracks of generations of Cannon Mountain skiers.

CANNON RACERS, INNKEEPERS AND MOUNTAIN MANAGERS

Since the earliest Cannon skiers hiked to the summit and schussed their way down, Cannon has been known as a skier's mountain: a place with plenty of good skiers and not a lot of fluff. Like the American ski pioneers who turned to the mountain seeking thrills and adventure, today's Cannon skiers come here, quite simply, to just ski—whether it's snowing or sleeting, fluffy powder or interminable ice, sunshiny calm or relentlessly windy. "There's something about Cannon," said former mountain manager Harry Reid. "It's an old mountain. The people who ski it year after year after year know when it's going to be great, know when it's going to be terrible. They're content to take the one run and bag it and come back [another day]. And if it rains, get a trash bag."[277]

The folks who have contributed to Cannon's development and evolution as a ski area are innumerable. They have included ski racers who honed their skills on Cannon's challenging trails, innkeepers and businesspeople whose vested interest in the ski area's success mandated direct participation in its development and countless employees—many who spent several decades working at Cannon—who have served as stewards of this piece of Franconia Notch State Park.

THE RACERS

From the Dow Academy boys of the 1930s to twenty-first-century superstar Bode Miller, Cannon's ski racing history is impressive. A handful of Olympians has passed through Cannon Mountain, beginning with John

Carleton, who competed in the first Winter Olympics in 1924, and Alec Bright, who raced in the 1936 Olympics, when alpine events were included for the first time.

Cannon kids Joan Hannah and Gordi Eaton raced in Olympic and FIS events in the 1960s. After winning the downhill competition in the Junior Nationals Championships in 1956 and 1957, Hannah competed in the 1960 and 1964 Olympics and the 1962 and 1966 FIS events, winning an FIS World Championship bronze medal in the Giant Slalom at Chamonix in '62. She also won six national giant slalom titles in the 1960s.[278]

Hannah grew up at her family's Ski Hearth Farm, where "the spirit and the atmosphere of racing permeated the household."[279] She learned to ski as a small child and was soon racing down the slopes at Cannon. "We would all be parked at the rope tow. And every time my folks took a trip up the tram, they'd look to see if there were still four kids there," said Joan of skiing with her three younger siblings at Cannon.[280] Sister Lucy was a junior USEASA champion, and brothers Sel Jr. and Frank both skied for Dartmouth. Sel Jr.

Joan Hannah competing in the 1964 U.S. Nationals at Winter Park, Colorado. *Courtesy Joan Hannah.*

was also on the U.S. Olympic Nordic team in 1964. Hannah's niece Eva Pfosi also raced for Dartmouth and the U.S. Ski Team.[281]

Joan Hannah became a skiing cover girl in the 1960s, appearing on the cover of *Ski* in 1960, prior to the Squaw Valley Olympics, and *Sports Illustrated* in 1962, preceding the FIS Championships. Following her retirement from the then strictly amateur national team in 1966—so stringent were the rules that she had to return the skis on which she won her FIS medal at season's end—Hannah became a certified ski instructor and spent twenty-six years in Vail, Colorado, teaching skiing in the winters and working as a potter in the summers. While at Vail, she competed in several Skiing Legends races. She returned to Ski Hearth Farm following Sel Hannah's death in 1991 to care for her mother and manage the farm.

Joan Hannah still lives in the family home above the farm, which was purchased by Bode Miller in 2005, and crafts pottery in her studio just down the country road. The former Olympian now teaches a "Flying 50s" class at nearby Loon Mountain for aspiring ski racers over the age of fifty. Hannah, who raced in the days of unforgiving bamboo gates, also takes a weekly racing class at Cannon, learning the more modern ski racing techniques that have come with breakaway gates and shorter, shapelier skis. She was elected to the U.S. National Ski Hall of Fame in 1978.

Gordi Eaton was also a member of the 1960 and '64 Olympic teams and the 1962 FIS team. He won the National Collegiate Athletic Association Downhill Championship in 1961, racing for Middlebury College in Vermont. After retiring from racing, he coached the U.S. team in the late 1960s, beginning when Bob Beattie was head coach, and later coached for Middlebury. Eaton also worked with Beattie as he established NASTAR and the World Pro Skiing tour. Eaton made a career in skiing, going on to work as a ski tester and developer for American ski maker K2 and as a sales representative for various ski clothing lines. He and his wife, Karen Budge Eaton, also a former U.S. Ski Team member, split their time between Middlebury and Lincoln, New Hampshire.

Eaton's parents, Steve and Peg, were among the Franconia area's original ski enthusiasts, skiing at Peckett's in the early days and becoming founding members of the Franconia Ski Club. "It was just natural that Steve and Peg's kids were going to go skiing. I just took to it. I love winter, and I love sliding down the mountain," Eaton said in 2010. He attributes his racing success to growing up at Cannon, where by necessity he learned to ski aggressively. "What a great place to grow up. It's a tough mountain to ski on," he said. "I just feel so damn lucky that I was in that atmosphere."[282]

Gordi Eaton, circa 1960. *Courtesy Joan Hannah.*

Of all the racers who have called Cannon their home hill, the most successful is Bode Miller. Miller grew up on the slopes of Cannon as a third-generation skier of the mountain. His grandparents, Jack and Peg Kenney, opened the Tamarack ski lodge in Easton in the 1940s and later started a tennis camp there, which the family continues to operate. Peg was a strong racer, narrowly missing a berth on the Olympic team in 1948. "She was reckless, especially for a young racer then," Bode said of his maternal grandmother in his autobiography. "She drove like a bank robber, drank whiskey from the bottle, loved to gamble, and was a kick-ass competitor."[283]

Mike and Peter "Bubba" Kenney, two of Jack and Peg's five children, both spent some time as pro ski racers. Mike has coached with the U.S. Ski Team, and he coached his nephew Bode's one-man ski team when Miller broke away from the national team to compete on his own during the winter of 2007–8.

That move was indicative of the independence Miller has become known for. He's often portrayed as a skier who follows his own path, even if that path diverges sharply from where others think it should go. Miller's unfettered approach to skiing has led to both innovation and more ski racing success than any other American has achieved. As a teenager in the mid-1990s, Miller introduced the racing world to shaped—or parabolic—skis before anyone else was racing on them. In the years since, Miller has garnered numerous ski racing accolades: the overall World Cup titles in 2005 and 2008; World Cup titles in the super combined, super G and giant slalom events; FIS World Championship gold medals in downhill, super G, giant slalom and combined; silver medals in the combined and giant slalom races at the 2002 Olympics in Salt Lake; and the trifecta—gold in super combined, silver in super G, bronze in downhill—in the 2010 Vancouver Olympics, Miller's fourth Games.[284]

Miller, who was home-schooled for several years in his early childhood, honed his racing skills from a young age, skiing top-to-bottom runs at Cannon while his contemporaries were stuck in school. "I knew I'd be an athlete in the same way other people decide to be artists or doctors or pilots when they're in college…by the time I was seven years old, in my mind I was a World Cup ski racer in training," Miller wrote in his autobiography.

Bode Miller skis with a slew of young fans at Cannon during the 2010 BodeFest, an annual fundraiser for Miller's Turtle Ridge Foundation. *Photo courtesy Paul Hayes/Record-Littleton.*

"I logged serious hours on the mountain. A few years running, I skied every day Cannon Mountain was open."[285]

A few years behind Bode came another Cannon skier who has found success on the world stage. Tyler Walker was born missing much of his spine and at age four had his legs amputated. His sense of adventure, however, remained intact, and Walker has achieved considerable success in the Paralympics, World Cup and X-Games. He's competed in two Paralympic Games (in Torino, Italy, in 2006 and Vancouver in 2010); won the International Paralympic Committee World Cup giant slalom title in 2006 and the downhill title in 2009; won national championship titles in giant slalom and slalom in 2008; earned gold medals in the 2009 and 2010 Mono Skier X event in the X-Games; and was crowned the Canadian National Champion in 2011.

Other racers who learned to ski at Cannon include the indomitable Diana Golden, who lost a leg to cancer at age twelve and continued to ski, capturing a gold medal and many hearts in the 1988 Olympics in Calgary, where disabled skiing was introduced as a demonstration sport.[286] Golden was inducted to the U.S. Ski Hall of Fame in 1997. Duncan Cullman raced briefly for the U.S. Ski Team and won a modified Inferno race on Mount Washington in 1969.[287] Courtney Calise and Caitlin Ciccone both spent time in recent decades on the U.S. Ski Team, and Ciccone was crowned U.S. National Giant Slalom Champion in 2006. Former Cannon Mountain skiers have also achieved success in telemark racing. Kelsey (Connors) Schmid-Sommers is a five-time U.S. Telemark National Champion, winning the title each year from 2006 to 2010, before retiring from competition.[288] Cannon kid Cory Snyder began racing for the U.S. National Telemark team in 2010.

With more youngsters discovering the joys of skiing at Cannon each winter and honing their skills on the mountain's challenging trails, Cannon's ski racing legacy promises to endure.

The Innkeepers

During the 1940s, '50s, and into the '60s, there was a core group of innkeepers who did much to foster Cannon as a ski center and to draw skiers to the area from afar. During this era, the Franconia Ski Club was heavily involved in marketing the area, and most local innkeepers were active members of the club. Peckett's, of course, attracted the earliest skiers. Other lodging accommodations followed, offering not only beds and meals but also plenty of fun. The innkeepers of today are surely a devoted bunch—you have to be to run an inn. But as John Jerome wrote in a 1977 *Skiing* article, in the early days, before snowmaking, grooming and Gore-Tex, things were different:

> *New Hampshire liquor laws were among the most conservative in the nation, there was no such thing as snowmaking, and the weather wasn't any more dependable then than it is now…Faced with a lodgeful [sic] of disgruntled skiers who had really gone to some trouble to get there, only to find poor—or no—snow on the mountain, the innkeepers quickly realized that they were It the moment the skiing no longer sufficed. Impromptu costume balls, a roulette wheel or two, a bent law here and there, and other adventures. No small quantities of booze were involved: If you couldn't keep the customers amused, then you could work at getting them unconscious.*[289]

There was a handful of ski lodges in town prior to World War II, including the Hannahs' Ski Hearth Farm and the Thorner House, as well as more established inns like Lovett's in Franconia, opened by Irish immigrants

A crowd gathers for fun during an annual Easter Parade in the 1950s. Jack Kenney is second from left, with Mary Cushing and Phil and Wody Robertson directly to his left. Peg Kenney is third from the right. *Charles Trask photo, NESM Collection.*

Charles and Ellen Lovett in the 1930s, and the Homestead in Sugar Hill, run by Enzo and Esther Serafini. The Kinsman Lodge, McKenzie's (now Franconia Inn) and the Caramat Terrace (now Sugar Hill Inn) were also open in the winter, and their proprietors had done much to promote skiing in the area from the start. After the war, many others appeared: Phil Robertson's Hillwinds, Jack and Peg Kenney's Tamarack, New York financier Tally Ruxton's Horse & Hound Inn, Dudley's Ski Barn run by Cannon ski patroller Jim Dudley, and Mittersill among them. The scene both on the hill and off was jovial.

"It was right after the Second World War, and everybody was just glad to be alive," said Chuck Lovett, whose father, Charlie, returned to Franconia after working in upscale kitchens and hotels in Springfield, Massachusetts, and New York City and then serving in the army during World War II. Charlie bought Lovett's Inn from his father after the war. "[The innkeepers] were all friends," said Chuck Lovett. "All those folks loved to party. They had a lot of fun."[290]

Accommodations ranged from the bunkhouse-type rooms at Dudley's and Ski Hearth Farm to the more refined atmosphere of Lovett's. But the fun was everywhere. Skiers—and their hosts—would travel from one ski lodge

Charlie and Mary Helen Lovett at the summit of Cannon, circa 1950s. *Charles Trask photo, courtesy Chuck Lovett.*

to the next after dark, creating a party trail. "There was always something crazy going on. It was really party time," said Joan Hannah, who likens the après ski scene of the 1940s and '50s to college fraternity house antics. "They skied hard all day and they partied hard all night."[291]

When ski conditions at Cannon were less than ideal, the innkeepers would either cart guests to snowier locales or get to work making things better. "Phil [Robertson] and Charlie [Lovett] and the others would climb the mountain with snow shovels and snowshoes and snow fences and work… far into the night if a storm promised new snow," Nicolas Howe wrote in *Skiing* magazine in 1981. "After supper at the inn, Phil would join his guests and start violent arguments about something else to keep their minds off the melting snow."[292]

Out-of-town skiers often became regulars at one inn or another. College students and young graduates found their fun at Ski Hearth or Dudley's. Ski writers lodged with journalist-cum-innkeeper Enzo Serafini and his wife, Esther, at the Homestead, telling tales into the night. The Hillwinds bar was a popular gathering spot— and the starting point for more than a few lasting marriages. Lovett's served up fine fare and employed Austrian and Swiss skiers in the bar, and Charlie Lovett would serve guests lunch slope side—set on a picnic table at the mountain with wine chilled in the snow. The Horse & Hound mixed the strongest drinks. Mittersill provided a touch of glamour—amidst the fun, of course.

Many of the innkeepers were also known for endearing personal traits.

Innkeeper and editor Enzo Serafini (center) with Hubert von Pantz and Sugar Hill resident Edwin MacEwan outside the Homestead Inn. *Enzo Serafini Collection.*

Sel and Paulie Hannah, sans shoes, dance at their Ski Hearth Farm during the 1940s.
Courtesy Joan Hannah.

Sel Hannah, besides being a terrific skier and skilled trail designer, was famous for taking his shoes off as the party got going. He would dance, drive and walk through the snow to the next party barefoot. Jack Kenney, a Dartmouth graduate and World War II veteran, was outrageously funny, telling jokes and spinning tall tales. "At the dinner table, he'd go on for an hour, just telling jokes. He'd make up these ridiculous stories that sounded like they were true, but you knew damn well that they weren't. They were made out of pure cloth," said Joe Cushing, who worked for Jack and Peg as a teenager.[293] "He was the front man, and my mom was the real workhorse," said Jo Kenney Miller of her parents. "[Tamarack was] a pretty wild and fun place."[294]

There were other inns and lodges, of course, some that continue to welcome guests in all seasons, although many of the lodges that opened specifically for skiers are gone now. While there are a few places today to grab a beer or dinner around town, the scene is not quite the same as it was in Cannon's early decades as a ski area. There are no costume balls or roulette wheels, no revelers wandering barefoot through the snow, no need for the innkeepers to schlep up the mountain in the dark of night to shovel in the ruts. The fun these days is tamer.

The Mountain Managers

In Cannon's history as a ski area, there have been many employees who have worked at the mountain for decades, making their careers as lift mechanics, on ski patrol in winter and trail crews in summer, loading chairlifts and conducting tramcars and doing whatever the managers of the mountain and state park needed. Some families include generations of Cannon workers—the Peabodys, of course, but also the Champagnes. Damus Sr., who learned to ski while a kitchen boy at Peckett's, helped construct the tramway in 1938 and worked as a ski patroller, tram conductor and lift mechanic for years after. His son, Damus Jr., grew up on Cannon and spent his working years as a mechanic, helping to construct Tram II.[295] There have been other families, too—Hunts and Roys, Whitcombs, Herberts and Balls.

Children who grew up on the mountain have returned from years away to find the same folks manning the lifts and roaming the base lodge. To endeavor to describe all of Cannon's longtime workers would take volumes. Through it all, there have been only eight managers.

When Roland Peabody died in 1950, his son, Roger, became the second manager of Cannon Mountain. Roger had learned to ski at Peckett's alongside his father, raced for Franconia's Dow Academy and the University of New Hampshire and worked in various positions at Cannon. He managed the mountain until 1954, when he became executive director of the USEASA. Roger Peabody was succeeded by Bill Norton, a salesman for the U.S. Rubber Company who lived in Sugar Hill.

Roger Peabody skiing above the Old Man of the Mountain for a publicity photo in 1948. *Courtesy Jere Peabody.*

137

Norton ran the ski area for twenty-five years, earning a reputation as a fair boss, able manager and marketer and a leader in the ski industry. He served as president of the Eastern Ski Area Operators Association, the National Ski Areas Association and the White Mountains Attractions Association and for many years chaired the New Hampshire Tramway Safety Board.

"He was well liked at Cannon Mountain and had a lot of respect from his people. But in terms of what he contributed to the industry and the respect that he had, it was nationwide. It was far, far broader than Cannon," said Phil Gravink, who spent a year as New Hampshire's "Ski Czar" and knew Norton well. "He was just very giving of time, a brilliant mind, a good chairman, a good speaker, outgoing, fun-loving, loyal to friends and the industry…just very steady."[296]

Norton administered considerable ski area growth at Cannon—including the 1967 World Cup races and the construction of Tram II in 1980. As superintendent of the entire Franconia Notch State Park, he was also responsible for helping to orchestrate numerous other events and details. Among these were two presidential visits: Dwight Eisenhower's 1955 trip to the Notch to commemorate the 175th anniversary of the Old Man of the Mountain's discovery, and Gerald Ford's campaign stop in New Hampshire's capital city, Concord, in 1976. Norton retired as manager in 1980, after overseeing the construction and opening of Tram II. But he remained at the mountain, spending several more winters as a lift attendant.

Norton's assistant manager for many years was Newt Avery, who had started at Cannon in the fall of 1937, when he worked on the tramway's construction.[297] He was assistant manager from the early 1950s until his death in 1968, preferring the second-in-command post to being the top boss. "He was a character," said Bill Roy, who worked at Cannon for decades and became mountain manager in 1999. "Newt would ski up, take his skis off and…start loading T-bars with you and chitchat…You never knew when you were going to see him…He'd be all over the place. You didn't have radios then—nobody could call you and tell you the boss was coming."[298]

When Avery died, Harry Reid was hired as assistant manager. Reid had grown up in Sugar Hill, worked loading T-bars at Cannon as a kid during World War II and had just returned to the area following a twenty-year career in the army. He brought to the job a good dose of military toughness. "Harry always told it like it was," said Roy. "I had a lot of respect for the man, and everybody else did…As much as he screamed and hollered, and as military as he was, the man had a heart of gold. And he taught me an awful lot."[299]

Reid became Cannon's fourth manager in 1980 and held the post for a decade. He was followed by Gary Whitcomb (no relation to the Gary Whitcomb for whom Gary's Trail is named), who had worked at the mountain for some time, primarily as an aerial lift mechanic, and managed the ski area during the brief era that New Hampshire had a director of ski operations—a "Ski Czar"—to oversee both Cannon and Sunapee.

When Whitcomb retired in 1995, another North Country native, Dick Andross, became manager. Andross grew up in nearby Lisbon and had raced for the Franconia Ski Club. He was later head coach of the FSC for ten years. He'd also worked for Sel Hannah, laying out a ski area in Pennsylvania, and spent a decade working in property management and mountain operations at Loon Mountain, just south of Cannon.

During the winter of 2000, Andross moved on to Burke Mountain in Vermont, where he became vice-president of operations. But he continues to live just down the road from Cannon's Peabody Slopes and is a trustee of the Roland Peabody Memorial Fund. Andross believes Cannon's inclusion within a state park—and its wild weather—set it apart from other ski areas:

Bill Roy (right), a longtime Cannon employee and manager, at the summit with New Hampshire governor John Lynch, circa 2005. *Courtesy Bill Roy.*

"Being part of the state parks system, the philosophy [at Cannon] has always been a little different…Traditions mattered. And history mattered…The employees all took a ton of pride in the place. There was just a general sense of stewardship."[300]

In 1999, Bill Roy became the seventh manager at Cannon. He'd spent the previous year working as the supervisor of state parks, but before then had been at Cannon since 1963, when he was a high school kid loading T-bars. Roy became a full-time mountain employee in 1969 and worked myriad jobs at the mountain—snowmaking, tramcar conductor, lift mechanic and assistant manager. "I love the park and the ski operation. I spent most of my life there," he said in 2010, four years after retiring from Cannon. "You sit in park headquarters and you look out…at Lafayette and Echo Lake on one side and the mountain and ski trails on the other. That was my office. How could you not like it?"[301]

John DeVivo was hired as general manager for the ski area and state park in 2007. With experience running other areas—a year at Attitash in New Hampshire and sixteen years at Sunday River in Maine—DeVivo brought new energy to Cannon. DeVivo and his team spent over $6 million between 2008 and 2011 on improvements from snowmaking and grooming—which he identified as priorities—to base area facilities that included a new pub, a new rental and repair shop, expanded seating for both cafeteria patrons and brown-baggers and a vastly expanded outside deck area. He also helped orchestrate the long-awaited reopening of Mittersill and the integration of that area with the Cannon Mountain operation.

"What we didn't do was change the overall culture and feel of Cannon. We want to remain a little rough around the edges, and we've done that," said DeVivo. "Everything we've done focuses on the experience, rather than the aesthetics."[302]

The aesthetic nature of Cannon Mountain is complex. Its beauty is in the magnificence of the mountain landscape within and around it, in the depth of its skiing history and in the people who have dedicated a part of themselves to the mountain. In many ways, the main challenge of managing Cannon Mountain as a ski area is the same in the twenty-first century as it was in 1938: finding a balance between attracting business and maintaining lifts and trails with the sometimes contradicting goal of preserving the natural character of Franconia Notch.

TIMELINE OF
CANNON EVENTS

1805	Old Man of the Mountain is discovered by surveyors in Franconia Notch.
1852	Profile House, a grand hotel, is built in Franconia Notch.
1882	Nansen Ski Club, the oldest continuous ski club in the United States, is founded in Berlin, New Hampshire.
1909	The Dartmouth Outing Club is founded.
1923	Profile House is destroyed by fire.
1927	The state purchases the 6,000-acre Franconia Notch property with assistance from the Society for the Protection of New Hampshire Forests. The Forest Society initially maintains title to the southern 913 acres, and the state controls the northern 4,331 acres, including Profile and Echo Lakes and Cannon Mountain. In September 1928, the Franconia Notch Forest Reservation and State Park is dedicated as a memorial to New Hampshire men and women who have served the country in times of war.
1928	The road through Franconia Notch is first kept open for winter travel.
1929	The ski school is established at Peckett's-on-Sugar Hill.
December 1930	Ski Club Hochgebirge is founded.

1931	The Boston & Maine Railroad begins snow train service on weekends from the city to New Hampshire mountain areas.
1932	The third Winter Olympics is held at Lake Placid, New York. Ski competition is limited to Nordic events. Construction of the Richard Taft Trail begins on Cannon Mountain, to be completed in 1933 by the Civilian Conservation Corps.
April 1933	The Franconia Ski Club is incorporated.
1933	Alec Bright of the Ski Club Hochgebirge proposes building an aerial tramway in New Hampshire.
1934	Ski trails in the Franconia area include the Richard Taft Trail, the Coppermine Trail, the Kinsman Trail, Peckett's slopes and the trail on Bald Mountain (across from the present-day Peabody base area).
1935	The state legislature approves construction of a tramway on Cannon Mountain, but no funding is appropriated. Manchester attorney and former Olympic skier John Carleton is named chairman of the Aerial Tramway Commission. The Coppermine Brook Trail connects with the Taft Trail; the Taft is improved.
1936	Alpine ski events are included for the first time in the Winter Olympics, held in Garmisch, Germany. Franconia teenagers Roger Peabody, Norwood Ball, Bertram Herbert and Bobby Clark give skiing demonstrations, under the direction of Sig Buchmayr, at Madison Square Garden during New York City's first Winter Sports Show.
1937	The state legislature approves a $250,000 bond for construction of the tramway at Cannon. James McLeod of Littleton is named chairman of the Aerial Tramway Commission. Roland Peabody is hired as manager of the tramway.
July 1937	Charles N. Proctor is hired to survey possible trails on Cannon. Sel Hannah designs the trails.
June 1938	The Cannon Mountain Aerial Tramway opens. Ski runs include Taft Slalom and the Cannon Mountain Trail, with the Taft Racecourse, Coppermine and

Tucker Brook Trails over the saddle. The Cannon and Taft Trails connect with the Fleitman Trail, a cross-country-style trail to bring skiers back to the tram's Valley Station. Winter tramway fare is ninety-five cents round-trip or sixty cents to ride up only. Ten-trip (one-way) books cost five dollars.

1939   The Tram Ravine Trail (later called simply Ravine), practice slopes near the Valley Station and Lookout Trail at the summit are added.

1941   The new Alpine lift T-bar opens at the top of Cannon Mountain, transporting skiers from three-thousand-foot elevation to the forty-one-hundred-foot summit. The Upper and Lower Hardscrabble Trails are cut. Ski trains arrive in Lisbon and Littleton each weekend from New York City ($11.80–$12.70 round-trip fare) and Boston ($4.00 round-trip fare).

1942   The Middle Hardscrabble Trail is cut.

Cannon's three trails from the summit, circa 1940: Cannon Mountain Trail, Ravine and Taft Slalom. The tramway was the only lift. *Charles Trask photo, NESM Collection.*

1942–1945	Cannon reduces its staff to a skeleton crew of eight during the United States' involvement in World War II. Several Cannon skiers join the service.
1945	The Mittersill ski area is opened by Austrian baron Hubert von Pantz.
1946	The U.S. Nationals downhill and slalom events for men and women are held on the Taft.
	The state approves $5,000 in Cannon improvements, including increasing the practice slope by the Valley Station of the tramway to ten acres, doubling length of the rope tow there to seven hundred feet and building a warming shelter. The Upper and Lower Hardscrabble Trails are connected.
October 1947	The Society for the Protection of New Hampshire Forests transfers the deed of the Flume Reservation

A rope tow serviced practice slopes—at what is now the Banshee Trail—near the tramway Valley Station during the 1940s and '50s. These were replaced by a T-bar in 1962. *Charles Trask photo, NESM Collection.*

	to the State of New Hampshire, bringing the Flume into the Franconia Notch State Reservation.
1947–1948	Sel Hannah and Ed Blood survey all Cannon trails to make improvements: Ravine Trail is widened, a fifteen-hundred-foot glade is built near the practice slope at the base and the seven-hundred-foot rope tow is doubled in length. The sundeck of the tram's Mountain Station is enclosed and enlarged.
1949	The Tramway and Easy Way (later named Vista Way) Trails are cut.
Winter 1949–1950	Paul Valar begins his twenty-plus year tenure as director of the Cannon and Mittersill ski schools. He is joined in this endeavor the following year by Paula Kann Valar, after their marriage in the summer of 1950.
1950	Roland Peabody dies and is succeeded by his son, Roger Peabody, as manager of the tramway and Franconia Notch property. The New Hampshire Aerial Tramway Commission is abolished by the state legislature, and all functions of the commission are transferred to the State Forestry and Recreation Commission. The Paulie's Folly Trail is cut.
1951	The Alpine lift T-bar is extended.
1953–1954	The Roland Peabody Memorial Slopes development is completed on Cannon at cost of $305,000, including five new trails (Red Ball, Lower Cannon, Turnpike, Zoomer and Lower Ravine), a lower T-bar and middle T-bar (with the existing upper T-bar, these connect new base area to summit) and a base lodge. Cannon has seventeen trails and six lifts.
1955	Roger Peabody resigns, and Bill Norton is hired as manager. Cannon hosts the National Alpine Ski Championships/Olympic Trials. A new forty-meter ski jump is constructed (in large part by the Franconia Ski Club) near the tram's Valley Station for the 1956 Junior Nationals.
1956	The FSC hosts the National Junior Alpine and Nordic Championships.
1958	The Upper T-bar (Alpine lift) is replaced. The National Collegiate Ski Championships are held at Cannon.

The Peabody T-Bar, installed in 1953, carried skiers from the new Peabody Base Area to the mid-mountain T-bar. Skiers could reach the summit by linking three T-bar rides from the base. *Warren Bartlett photo.*

1961   The State of New Hampshire creates a Department of Resources and Economic Development, including a Division of Parks and Recreation. The legislature authorizes a $9 million bond issue for expansion of the state parks system, with millions allocated to the Cannon and Mount Sunapee ski areas. The Tramway, Vista Way, Cannon Link and Middle Cannon Trails are widened and improved. A one-day lift ticket at Cannon costs $5.50; a season pass, $90.00.

1962   A new $651,000 development on Cannon begins with the creation of the Gary's, Rocket, Avalanche, Banshee (at Valley Station practice slopes), Gremlin, Toss-up and Skylight Trails. The Upper Ravine, Taft Slalom and Upper Hardscrabble Trails are improved. A T-bar is installed on Banshee slope (formerly a rope tow). Two

	double chairs—Zoomer and Peabody (from the base area to the bottom of the upper T-bar)—are installed.
1963	The Middle and Lower Hardscrabble and By-Pass Trails are improved, and the Peabody base lodge is enlarged. Cannon has twenty-four trails and eight lifts. The National Cross-Country and Nordic Combined Championships are held at Cannon.
1965	A second upper T-bar is installed adjacent to the existing T-bar.
1966	The Vista Way and Middle By-Pass Trails and the corner into Avalanche Trail are redesigned for the North American Alpine Championships downhill course at a cost of $12,000.
1967	Cannon hosts the North American Alpine Championships, which are the first World Cup races in the United States.
1969	A new $544,000 snowmaking system is installed, with a capacity to cover thirty-five acres. Cannon has a

Cannon Mountain manager Bill Norton (left) and Jere Peabody clear heavy snowfall from the new snowmaking guns during the snowy winter of 1969. *Dorothy Crossley photo.*

	record season— November 16, 1968, through April 21, 1969—with 285 inches of natural snowfall and 141 days skiing. The Eastern Alpine Championships are held at Cannon.
1972	The new $328,000 Peabody Base Lodge opens. A $20,000 "New Peabody" double chairlift replaces the Peabody T-bar. (Cannon employees and skiers dub this lift the "Hong Kong" chair, and it is referenced on various trail maps over the years as the New Peabody, Hong Kong and Gremlin chair.)
1975	Snowmaking capacity increases to fifty acres.
1976	The Franconia Ski Club moves into its new headquarters, Ernie's Haus, donated by the Glaessel family and built at the bottom of Gary's Trail.
1980	The original tramway is replaced with the modern version at a cost of $4.7 million. Capacity increases from twenty-seven to eighty passengers per car. Cannon manager Bill Norton retires, and Norton's assistant manager, Harry Reid, is hired as Cannon's fourth manager.
1982	The New England Ski Museum opens adjacent to the tram's Valley Station, with Paul Valar as president.
1983	Snowmaking is extended to the top of the mountain, increasing coverage to eighty acres. Lifts include the tram, three double chairs, two T-bars and a modified rope tow.
1984	The Mittersill ski area is closed (the majority of land containing ski slopes would be transferred to the state in 1989). The Zoomer chairlift is upgraded from a double chair to a triple.
1989	The State Division of Ski Operations is created (to be abolished in 1996).
1990	The Upper T-bars are replaced by the Cannonball Express quad chairlift. The Profile Trail is cut (later named Cannonball).
1993	With the rising popularity of snowboarding, Cannon creates a six-hundred-foot half pipe and allows unrestricted snowboarding. The mountain gets a new winchcat groomer.

The Zoomer chairlift, serving the "front five" trails, opened as a double in 1962 and was upgraded to a triple chairlift in 1984. *Dorothy Crossley photo*.

1998   Mount Sunapee, the only other state-owned ski area in New Hampshire, is leased to the Okemo Mountain Company, with lease payments to the state funding $6 million of expansion and improvements at Cannon. State Department of Resources and Economic Development commissioner Robb Thomson, in his recommendation to maintain state control of Cannon, says, "Cannon is an integral part of Franconia Notch State Park, and Franconia Notch State Park is the crown jewel of the park system. Cannon cannot be separated without causing major disruption within the park system."[303] (Debate on the benefits and downfalls of leasing Cannon continues to crop up in the state legislature.) The state legislature establishes the Cannon Mountain Advisory Commission, which accepts the master plan for Cannon improvements developed by Sno-engineering.

1999 Improvements include installation of the new high-speed Peabody Express quad chairlift (to replace the old double), the Eagle Cliff triple chairlift (to replace the Hong Kong chair), the Brookside triple chair and construction of the Brookside Learning Center.

2003 New development includes the creation of a beginner/intermediate network of seven trails (Rabbit Path, Turkey Trot, Moose Alley, Deer Run, Bear Paw, Coyote Crossing and a revamped Fleitman Trail; more trails would be added later) and

Paul and Paula Valar's daughter, Christina Valar Breen, and granddaughter, Annina Valar Breen, rode the first chair when the Mittersill double chair opened on January 1, 2011. *Photo courtesy Greg Keeler/Cannon Mountain.*

the Tuckerbrook quad chairlift, all set between the Peabody slopes and the base of Mittersill. Lakeview Glade is opened between the Rocket and Zoomer Trails. Kinsman Glade and the Tramline Trail are opened. The "Old Peabody Lodge" is expanded and renamed Notch View Lodge. Cannon lists fifty-five trails and nine lifts.

2005   The Summit Station of the tram is renovated.

2009   The Tramline Trail is renamed D.J.'s Tramline Trail. The Peabody Base Lodge is renovated and expanded. The Mittersill slopes are reopened as the "backcountry area" (no lift service, snowmaking or grooming) and incorporated into Cannon following a long-awaited land transfer between the state park and the U.S. Forest Service.

2011   The new $3 million Mittersill double chair opens along the old chair lift line at "Mittersill Terrain Area," offering the first lift access to Mittersill since 1984. Cannon lists seventy-two trails, plus Mittersill terrain, for a total of twenty-three miles—or 264 acres—of skiing.

AFTERWORD

Skiing today is in many ways enormously different than it was when the first hardy souls trudged up Cannon Mountain seeking the thrill of descent. But in this era of high-speed lifts and high-tech ski equipment, pricey lift tickets and cushy lodges, the adventurous spirit of American skiing's pioneers is alive and well on the slopes of Cannon Mountain. That spirit glows in the smallest skiers, who duck into hidden glades wherever they find them. It rides on the shoulders of racers seeking the speed that first attracted so many to the sport. It clings to skiers joyfully descending the mountain, following the tracks of those who have skied before them.

New skiers come to the mountain each winter, joining the people who have called Cannon home for many years. Some of them find something at Cannon that John Carleton and Alec Bright, Roland Peabody and Kate Peckett and numerous others discovered decades ago—the simple, pure exhilaration of sliding downhill—and they become part of Cannon's long history.

Developed as one of the country's first ski areas, Cannon Mountain has become one of several hundred now operating throughout the United States. From a few dozen winter employees, it has grown to some five hundred paid and volunteer workers each winter. From a single, winding trail, the ski area has spawned six dozen ski runs. From the skiing dreams of a few have been born the joyful turns of multitudes.

The people who helped establish Cannon Mountain and Franconia as a ski center in the 1930s looked to the mountain and the sport as an economic stimulus, and it continues to be an important part of the town's economic

The trails of Cannon Mountain and Mittersill (right) as viewed from Franconia in 2011. *Author photo.*

landscape. They looked to the mountain and the sport as a way to find beauty and freedom in the long months of winter, and skiing at Cannon—within the confines of a state park and bordered by National Forest land—remains as beautiful and free as anywhere.

Within this ongoing story are the skiers whose parents or grandparents discovered and came to love Cannon years ago. A few have Cannon pedigrees reaching even further back. Many winter days, the slopes of Cannon contain the happy and skillful turns of young, fifth-generation Cannon skiers, the great-great-grandchildren of Charles Lovett Sr., Roland Peabody and a handful of others. Not many ski areas in America have such a long lineage.

That is a part of what makes Cannon a special place to the people who ski there. It is an old mountain—and modern. It is lift-serviced—and backcountry. It can be beautiful or harsh, gentle or daring, rolling and twisting or fast and straight. The mountain's story is long: it resonates with history and hints of skiing legends yet to come.

ACKNOWLEDGEMENTS

W riting this book has been both a challenge and a joy, and I have been assisted by an array of people who have offered research assistance, opinions, recollections and encouragement.

My foremost thanks must be given to the folks at the New England Ski Museum (NESM), which sits at the base of Cannon Mountain in a tiny building filled with a vast knowledge of ski history. NESM executive director Jeff Leich has supported the idea of a book on Cannon since I first mentioned it back in 2003. His encouragement, insight, understanding of ski history and research guidance have been invaluable. Linda Bradshaw, Kay Kerr, Karin Martel, Donna Kaye Erwin and board members John Allen and Jeremy Davis have offered useful suggestions and genuine enthusiasm for the project along the way.

Thanks to Rebecca Brown, who encouraged me to write Cannon Mountain stories when she was my newspaper editor at the start of my career as a writer. Thanks to Lyn Bixby for teaching me to get to the point and that the most interesting part of most any story is the people involved. And thanks to Steve Morse, who has skied at Cannon for more than four decades and who one day in 2010, on the Cannonball chairlift, asked, "Who the heck was Taft, anyway?" thus inspiring me to finally write what I know of Cannon's history.

Thanks are also due the folks at The History Press who have guided me through this process, especially Jeff Saraceno, who answered my endless questions along the way, and Jaime Muehl, who reviewed the manuscript to ensure that *T*s were crossed and *I*s dotted.

Whatever pep and color is in these pages is thanks to the many people who have shared their memories and experiences of Cannon with me. These conversations ranged from a few minutes to several hours and have happened over the phone, on chairlifts, in living rooms and just around town. Mickey Libby, Roger Peabody, Paul Valar and Ray Martin are no longer with us, and I'm grateful to have talked with each of them.

Many have shared knowledge, documents and photographs, including Joan Hannah, Jere and Nancy Peabody, Jennifer Peabody Gaudette, Joel Peabody, Bob Ball, Bill Roy, Dick Andross, Harry Reid, Trevor Hamilton, Gordi Eaton, Bob Beattie, Joe Cushing, Rich Millen, Kim Cowles, Phil Branch, Peggy Branch, Beth and Gary Harwood, Jack McGurin, Anita and Bob Craven, Stefanie Valar, Christina Valar Breen, Marcia Graham, Dorothy Crossley, Lois Bijolle, Lynn Bishop, Rich and Martha McLeod, George and Nancy MacNeil, Phil Gravink, Margie Norton, Dick Hamilton, Ruth Taylor, Jo Miller, Wody Robertson, Bunny Nutter, Chuck Lovett, Greg Anthony, Bonnie Van Slyke, R.J. Lyman, Chet and Sue Thompson, Kathy and Red McCarthy and Dolly McPhaul.

Kitty Holman Bigelow of the Sugar Hill Historical Museum and Barbara Holt and Amy Bahr of the Franconia Heritage Museum were most obliging, as was ski historian Allen Adler. Barbara Serafini generously loaned photo albums and scrapbooks from her father's collection for my perusal.

Jane Cloran and Sybil Carey at Franconia's Abbie Greenleaf Library helped me track down old records from the New Hampshire State Archives and State Library. State archivist Frank Mevers suggested sources that were helpful in my research. Lee Wilder of the New Hampshire Geological Survey, Amy Bassett in the New Hampshire Division of Parks and John DeVivo, Greg Keeler, Bill Mead and Bruce Sullivan at Cannon Mountain also fielded questions.

Paul Hayes, Ellen Edersheim and Karl Stone provided photographic assistance; Paul also reviewed several chapters and tendered helpful advice.

Kathy McCarthy faithfully read every chapter as it was written and has graciously reviewed and suggested alterations to several drafts. My husband, David McPhaul, was also an early reader of various drafts of this book. He has been an invaluable copyeditor, fact checker, idea man, website designer and willing cheerleader throughout the process of creating this book. I am so very thankful for his support in this endeavor and many others.

I am indebted to each of these people and to many other friends and acquaintances who have offered encouragement along the way.

NOTES

Introduction

1. Robert P. Allen, "Ski Ability, Not Glamor [*sic*], Important on Cannon Mountain's Tricky Trails," *Boston Globe*, December 14, 1941.
2. Lee Wilder, New Hampshire Geological Survey, e-mail correspondence with author, March 24, 2011.
3. D.E. Glidden, *Weatherwise Magazine*, August 1974.
4. Johnson Hancock, *Saving the Great Stone Face*, 71–73.
5. Allen, *From Skisport to Skiing*, 107, 147.

Peckett's-on-Sugar Hill

6. Stephen Winship, "Peckett's Peppy Pioneers Broke a Lasting Trail," photocopy of article from Park Headquarters files at Cannon Mountain, undated.
7. Ray Martin and Katharine Holman Bigelow, personal interview by author, November 29, 2010.
8. Adler, *Peckett Mystique*.
9. Ibid.
10. Jay, *Ski Down the Years*, 77.
11. Norwood Ball, audio recording of interview by Ann Spaulding, October 14, 1979, New England Ski Museum (NESM).
12. Jay, *Ski Down the Years*, 127.
13. Donald Moffatt, "Peckett's," *New Yorker*, November 25, 1933.

14. Peckett's-on-Sugar Hill flyer, 1935–36, Enzo Serafini Collection; Ray Martin, personal interview with author, December 19, 2010.
15. Peckett's-on-Sugar Hill flyer.
16. B. Altman & Co. advertisement, *New Yorker*, November 28, 1935.
17. *Courier* [Littleton, NH], "Peckett's Had Enviable Reputation As Resort," December 25, 1969, 2D.

THE RICHARD TAFT TRAIL

18. Moffatt, "Peckett's."
19. New England Ski Museum exhibit at Cannon Mountain Tramway Mountain Station, winter 2010–11.
20. Charles N. Proctor, "New Ski Trails," *Appalachia*, December 1933, 602.
21. Roger Williams, "Major Eastern Mountain Racing Trails," *American Ski Annual and Skiing Journal* (1952).
22. Johnson Hancock, *Saving the Great Stone Face*, 30.
23. Program, "Third Annual Downhill Championship Race of the United States Eastern Amateur Ski Association," March 18, 1934, NESM 1990L.12.21.
24. Proctor, "New Ski Trails," 600.
25. Jeffrey R. Leich, "Winter Work: The CCC and New England Skiing," *Journal of the New England Ski Museum*, (Autumn 2004): 7.
26. Meghan McCarthy, "Taft Trail Offers a Glimpse into Ski History," *Courier*, March 3, 2004, 1C, 14C.
27. A.H.B., "Richard Taft Trail," *Ski Bulletin*, February 17, 1933, 7.
28. Carl E. Shumway, "New Hampshire Leads the Nation," *Sportsman*, December 1933, 34–36, NESM 1984L.17.9.
29. Norwood Ball, interview by Ann Spaulding, October 14, 1979, NESM.
30. Ibid.; Bunny Nutter, telephone interview with author, July 12, 2010.
31. 1946 U.S. National Downhill, Slalom and Combined Ski Championship results, Franconia Ski Club Collection.
32. *Courier*, "Ski Fatality," February 18, 1946.
33. Norwood Ball interview.

ALEXANDER BRIGHT AND THE SKI CLUB HOCHGEBIRGE

34. "Ski Club Hochgebirge," SCH website, hochgebirge.org/introduction/index.html.
35. *The Ski Club Hochgebirge 1931–1938*, club history (1938), 8.
36. *The Ski Club Hochgebirge 1931–1981*, club history (1981), 27–28.
37. hochgebirge.org/members/active_members.html.

38. *The Ski Club Hochgebirge 1931–1981*, 17.

39. Leich, *Over the Headwall*.

40. Undated news clipping, Hochgebirge files.

41. Marvin Chandler, "Sherburne and His Trail," *Skiing Heritage*, March 2005, 5.

42. Robert Sullivan, "To Race Or Not To Race? At Inferno Time, That's the Enduring Question," *Sports Illustrated*, April 4, 1983, 122.

43. *The Ski Club Hochgebirge 1931–1981*, 12–14.

44. Cameron Bright, telephone interview with author, November 4, 2004.

45. Ibid.

46. "Minnie" Dole, "Memories of My Earliest Skiing Days in Stowe," photocopy of typescript in George Wesson Papers, NESM, p. 3.

47. Norwood Ball, notes on Charles Trask photos, 1981, NESM, L80.34.1.

48. Roger Peabody, personal interview by author, May 20, 2004.

49. R.P.B. and John P. Carleton, "Aerial Tramway on Cannon Mountain," *Appalachia*, November 1935, 459.

50. Cameron Bright, telephone interview.

51. *The Ski Club Hochgebirge 1931–1938*, 13.

52. Cameron Bright interview.

Cannon Mountain Aerial Tramway

53. International Skiing History Association, "Timeline of Important Ski History Dates," www.skiinghistory.org/historicdates.html.

54. Jeffrey R. Leich, "Eastern Inspirations: The Impact of the Northeast on National Skiing," *Journal of the New England Ski Museum* (Spring 2007): 11.

55. Jean M. Greiner, "An Early Colorado Gondola," *Colorado Magazine* (Summer 1973): 196–206.

56. Edward Place, "Ski Club Hochgebirge Urges Aerial Cableways in N.E.," *Boston Evening Transcript*, December 9, 1933.

57. Ibid.

58. Alexander Bright, "Downhill Only," *Ski Annual*, 1934, 33.

59. *Appalachia*, The American-Bleichert-Zuegg on Cannon Mountain, N.H.," June 1938, 125; "Illustrated Story of the Cannon Mountain Aerial Passenger Tramway," 1948, 21.

60. Leich, "Eastern Inspirations," 11.

61. Alexander Bright, "Survey of Possible Aerial Tramway Locations," July 25, 1934, State of New Hampshire Archives.

62. "Illustrated Story ," 1939, 14–16.

63. *Manchester Union*, "Tramway Contract Awarded to Worcester, Mass., Firm," August 25, 1937.

64. *Concord Monitor*, "CCC Crews to Aid on Aerial Tramway Work," August 25 1937.

65. *Courier*, "Cannon Mountain Celebrates 70 Years," July 9, 2008, A14.

66. Cannon Mountain Scrapbook 1: 1935–1938, NESM.

67. *Appalachia*, "Illustrated Story," 21.

68. *Courier*, "Photographers Have Field Day at Preview of Canon Mt. Tramway," June 23, 1938, 1.

69. Ibid.

70. *Courier*, "New Cannon Mt. Aerial Tramway Christened with Echo Lake Water," June 30, 1938, 1, 4.

71. "Cannon's Tram Nearly Three Decades Old; Its History Recalled," press release issued by New Hampshire Division of Economic Development, March 1967.

72. *Courier*, "Popular Aerial Tramway Carries Couple to Wedding on Cannon Mountain," July 7, 1938, 1.

73. Jere Peabody, personal interview by author, July 26, 2010.

74. Ibid.

75. Peter Clark, personal interview by author, January 17, 2008.

76. Ray Martin, personal interview by author, July 21, 2010.

77. "Tramway This Winter," brochure for Cannon Mountain, 1938, NESM 2010.038.008.

78. *Courier*, "Official Investigation Today into Tragic Mishap on Tram," March 14, 1963, 1.

79. *Courier*, "Salvage Operations Now Underway at Cannon Site," March 21, 1963, 1.

80. *Courier*, "Will Obtain New Cable Car for Cannon Mt. Tramway Use," March 28, 1963, 1 & 4.

81. "Franconia Notch State Park Dedication Program Cannon Mountain Aerial Tramway II," May 24, 1980, 5–8.

82. Jack Colby, "Nearly 5,000 at Weekend Dedication of New Cannon Tramway," *Courier*, May 29, 1980, 1.

83. "Franconia Notch State Park Dedication Program," 2.

Roland Peabody

84. *Courier*, "Roland E. Peabody Dies Suddenly Following Seizure at Tramway," February 2, 1950, 4.

85. Ibid.; Roger Peabody, personal interview by author, May 20, 2004.

86. U.S. Eastern Amateur Ski Association, professional certificate to Roland Peabody, February 1935, NESM.

87. *Ski Bulletin*, "Ski Teachers Examination," December 9, 1938, 8.

88. http://www.nh.gov/nhinfo/stgovt.html.

89. Ray Martin, personal interview by author, July 21, 2010.

90. Jeffrey R. Leich, "The National Ski Patrol and Ski Patrolling in America," *Journal of the New England Ski Museum* (Summer 2008): 4.

91. Sel Hannah, "Notes on the Franconia Ski Club," December 1984, Franconia Ski Club Collection.

92. Joan Hannah, personal interview with author, September 30, 2003.

93. *Boston Herald*, "Franconia Gives Recreational Skiers a Break in Special Races," February 15, 1942, Enzo Serafini Collection.

94. Tap Goodenough, "Good Skiing Despite Heavy Rain Storms," *Boston American*, March 12, 1942, Enzo Serafini Collection.

95. Jere Peabody, telephone interview with author, August 8, 2008.

96. Joel Peabody, telephone interview with author, August 11, 2008.

97. *White Mountain Outlook*, "White Mountain Sketches," August 28, 1941, 4.

98. Jennifer Gaudette, telephone interview by author, August 9, 2010.

CANNON MOUNTAIN SKI PATROL

99. "About NSP," National Ski Patrol, http://www.nsp.org/about/about. aspx; Ken Boothroyd, audiotape of interview with Arthur March, September 27, 1988, NESM.

100. Jere Peabody, personal interview by author, July 26, 2010; Jere Peabody, telephone interview by author, August 8, 2008.

101. Ken Boothroyd, audiotape of interview.

102. Jere Peabody and Rich Millen, personal interview by author, July 26, 2010.

103. Ken Boothroyd, audiotape of interview.

104. *Boston Globe*, "Good Powder Snow Gives Week-End Skiers Good Sport," January 29, 1943.

105. Ken Boothroyd, audiotape of interview; Bob Ball, personal interview by author, July 5, 2010; Frank Elkins, "Deep Snow Awaits Franconia Skiers," *New York Times*, January 17, 1943.

106. Ken Boothroyd, audiotape of interview; Leah Cole and Shirley Campbell, audiotape of interview with Dick March, May 15, 1984, NESM.

107. Ken Boothroyd, audiotape of interview.

108. Jere Peabody, personal interview.

109. Bob Ball, personal interview by author, July 5, 2010.

110. Jere Peabody, personal interview.

111. Austin Macauley, "History of the Professional Ski Patrol Association," 1967.

112. "The Larry Collins Award," PSPA website, http://www.pspa.org.

113. Rich Millen, personal interview by author, July 26, 2010.

114. William Mead, telephone interview by author, August 9, 2010.

SEL HANNAH AND SNO-ENGINEERING

115. Nils Ericksen, notes to Paulie Hannah, October 11, 1991.

116. Susan Neidlinger McLane, "Sel Hannah" (eulogy), September 14, 1991.

117. Sel Hannah, transcript of interview by Ann Spaulding, November 14, 1979, NESM.

118. Sel Hannah, biographical notes, undated, NESM.

119. Ibid.

120. Ibid.

121. Nils Ericksen, notes to Paulie Hannah, October 11, 1991.

122. Ted Farwell, "A Tribute to Mr. Sel Hannah," January 11, 1989.

123. Joe Cushing, personal interview by author, May 10, 2010.

124. "Sno-engineering, Inc.," overview of company, typescript, no author, no date, NESM, 2001.164.002A.

125. Joe Cushing, personal interview.

126. Sel Hannah, transcript of interview.

127. Joe Cushing, personal interview.

128. SE Group timeline, e-mailed to the author by Claire Humber, September 14, 2010.

129. Peg Branch, telephone interview by author, November 11, 2010.

130. David Rowan, "Some thoughts on Jim Branch (1929–1991), *Ski Area Management*, May 1991, insert.

131. *Snomass Sun*, "James Branch, Ski Resort Designer, Dies," May 1, 1991, 2.

132. Peg Branch, telephone interview by author, November 11, 2010.

133. Linda McGoldrick, "Sno-Engineering—Reaching the Summit," *New Hampshire Premier*, March 1991, 9.

134. "Ford's…'Feel The Difference,'" *Snow.e Times* (Winter 1994): 1.

135. Meghan McCarthy, "Cannon Has New Lift, Trails, Revamped Lodge," *Courier*, November 19, 2003, 1A, 10A.

136. "A Brief Tour of Sno-engineering History," *Snow.e Times* (n.d.): 2; SE Group timeline.

137. Sel Hannah, transcript of interview by Ann Spaulding, November 14, 1979, NESM.

WARTIME SKIING AND POST–WORLD WAR II DEVELOPMENT

138. *Concord Monitor*, "Tramway Not to Be Closed at Cannon Mt.," January 22, 1943.

139. *New Hampshire Public Recreation Areas*, booklet issued by the state Forestry and Recreation Department and the State Planning and Development

Commission, 1942, New Hampshire State Library, Concord, New Hampshire, 917.42 N534pr 1942 C.3.

140. *Concord Monitor*, "Tramway Not To Be Closed At Cannon Mt.," January 22, 1943.

141. Franconia Notch Area, "Summary of Activities and Accomplishments to April 1, 1942," Enzo Serafini Collection.

142. Tap Goodenough, "Cannon Mountain Tramway Reveals Big Skiing Boom," *Boston Evening American*, January 8, 1942.

143. Frank Elkins, "Deep Snow Awaits Franconia Skiers," *New York Times*, January 17, 1943.

144. *Concord Monitor & New Hampshire Patriot*, "Cannon Mountain Now Trains Ski Troopers," February 8, 1943.

145. *Worcester Telegram*, "Ski Coach Father of Triplets," January 27, 1942.

146. Norwood Ball, personal interview by Ann Spaulding, October 14, 1979, NESM.

147. Jeffrey R. Leich, "New Hampshire and the Emergence of an American Ski Industry," *Historical New Hampshire* (Fall 2009): 94.

148. *Cannon Mountain Chronology*, sent via e-mail to author by Amy Bassett, New Hampshire Department of Resources and Economic Development, May 19, 2010.

149. Sel Hannah, biographical notes, undated, NESM; *Franconia Notch Reservation Study and Report*, issued by the New Hampshire State Planning and Development Commission, March 30, 1942, New Hampshire State Library 917.422 N535 C.3.

150. *Franconia Notch Reservation Study and Report*.

151. House Bill No. 405 Hearing, April 22, 1953, NESM, 2001.164.002E.

152. Ibid.; Reg Abbott, "Little Incident Stirs Big Plans to Regain Skiing Leadership for N.H.," *Manchester Union*, October 9, 1950, 16.

153. Henry Crawford, "New Hampshire Joins the Parade," *American Ski Annual and Skiing Journal*, 1954, 57–61.

154. *Littleton Courier*, "Cannon Mountain Sets Income Record As 4,000 Ski New Area, Older System," February 4, 1954.

155. New Hampshire State Planning & Development Commission, *Winter Facilities Development Committee—Report to the 1961 N.H. Legislature*, April 19, 1961.

156. Ibid.

157. Ralph V. White, "Mount Snow—Two Double Chair-Lifts Ready—And Five To Go!," *American Ski Annual and Skiing Journal* (1955): 39.

158. John Jerome, "Cannon: Big Gun or Cap Pistol," *Skiing*, December 1969, 102, 144–48.

159. Ibid.

MITTERSILL

160. Von Pantz, *No Risk, No Fun!*, 120.

161. Ibid., 133.

162. Ibid., 69.

163. Ibid., 35–38, 64, 111.

164. Ibid., 35; Crossley, *Take My Picture*, 58.

165. Von Pantz, *No Risk, No Fun!*, 133; Hubert von Pantz, transcript of personal interview by Mr. March, January 24, 1981, NESM.

166. *Manchester Union*, "Chalet Village Planned at Franconia," January 20, 1940, 1, 3.

167. Von Pantz, *No Risk, No Fun!*, 134; undated Mittersill/Franconia Lodge brochure.

168. Hubert von Pantz, transcript of personal interview by Mr. March, January 24, 1981, NESM.

169. Crossley, *Take My Picture*, 58.

170. Henry Moore, "Mittersill Ski Area Almost Ready for Altitude Open Slope Running," news clip (no publication name), December 6, 1946, Franconia Ski Club Collection.

171. Crossley, *Take My Picture*, 59; Von Pantz, *No Risk, No Fun!*, 141–43.

172. Von Pantz, *No Risk, No Fun!*, 142–43.

173. Paula Valar, transcript of interview by Edie Swift, September 9, 1986, NESM; Paul Valar, personal interview by author, June 2, 2004.

174. Paula Valar, transcript of interview.

175. Maurice M'Quillen, "The Mittersill: Continental Atmosphere in New Hampshire Mountains," *New Hampshire Sunday News*, March 30, 1952, 13.

176. Crossley, *Take My Picture*, 63.

177. *Harper's Bazaar*, "Skiing at Franconia," December 1941, 141–42.

178. Crossley, *Take My Picture*, 62-63.

179. Sel Hannah, "Appraisal of the Mittersill Ski Area," May 20, 1959, NESM.

180. Crossley, *Take My Picture*, 69.

181. Von Pantz, *No Risk, No Fun!*, 236; Crossley, *Take My Picture*, 91; http://www.nelsap.org/nh/mittersill.html.

182. Crossley, *Take My Picture*, 83, 112, 125.

183. James McLaughlin, Mittersill Alpine Inn director of operations, to Mittersill chalet owners, December 6, 1981, Marcia Graham's files.

184. Gene Murphy, Mittersill Alpine Inn manager, to Mittersill season pass holders, fall 1978, Marcia Graham files; Mittersill Association of Chalet Owners board, to MACO members, fall 1982, Marcia Graham files; J.H. Wetenhall, Mittersill president, to Mittersill chalet owners, October 21, 1983, Marcia Graham files.

185. "Mittersill History," Cannon Mountain, http://www.cannonmt.com/mittersill.html.

186. Ibid.

187. Robert Blechl, "Mittersill Lift Project Advances," *Littleton Record*, July 16, 2009, 12.

Paul and Paula Valar and the Transformation of Ski Instruction

188. Ford K. Sayre, "The Certification of Ski Teachers Under the U.S.E.A.S.A.," *American Ski Annual*, 1938–39, 146.

189. Ford V. Sayre and Charles N. Proctor, "Certification of Ski Teachers by the United States Eastern Amateur Ski Association," *Appalachia*, December 1938, 264–67.

190. E. John B. Allen, *Teaching & Technique: A History of American Ski Instruction*, EPSIA Educational Foundation, 1987, 19–26.

191. Sel Hannah, "Notes on the Franconia Ski Club (up to the 1960s)," December 1984, Franconia Ski Club Collection.

192. Allen, *Teaching & Technique*, 19–26.

193. *Philadelphia Record*, "Franconia Had First Ski School," December 24, 1939, Enzo Serafini Collection.

194. *Harper's Bazaar*, "Skiing at Franconia," December 1941, 141–42.

195. Robert P. Allen, "Outstanding Instructors Launch Village Ski School at Franconia," *Boston Globe*, January 6, 1942.

196. Roger Peabody, transcript of interview with Harry Stearns, November 28, 1980, NESM.

197. Stefanie Valar, *Paul Valar resume*, July 12, 2005.

198. Paula Kann Valar, transcript of interview by Edie Swift, September 9, 1986, NESM.

199. Ibid.

200. Franconia Ski Club Board of Governors letter to Paul Valar (c/o Paula Kann), June 13, Franconia Ski Club Collection.

201. Paula Kann Valar, transcript of interview by Edie Swift, September 9, 1986, NESM.

202. Paul Valar, personal interview by author, June 2, 2004.

203. Stefanie Valar, telephone interview by author, June 29, 2008.

204. Paul Valar, personal interview.

205. Stefanie Valar, *Paul Valar Resume*, July 12, 2005.

206. Kim Cowles, personal interview by author, September 30, 2010.

207. Gary Harwood, telephone interview by author, January 5, 2010.

208. Jack McGurin, email message to author, January 5, 2011.

209. Paul Valar, personal interview.

THE FRANCONIA SKI CLUB

210. *Manchester Union*, "Club Formed to Boom Region of Franconia Notch," April 10, 1933.

211. Franconia Ski Club Charter, April 21, 1933, Franconia Ski Club Collection.

212. Ibid.

213. *Manchester Union*, "Club Formed to Boom Region of Franconia Notch," April 10, 1933.

214. *Courier*, "Ski Club Backs Aerial Tramway," April 5, 1934.

215. Mrs. Henry A. Dodge Scrapbook, Enzo Serafini Collection.

216. *Time*, "Sport: Indoor Winter," December 21, 1936, http://www.time.com/time/magazine/article/0,9171,757219-1,00.html.

217. Agreement Between the Franconia Ski Club and the Division of Parks of the State of New Hampshire, January 2, 1964.

218. Franconia Ski Club, Minutes of Club Meeting, Meeting of October 9, 1940, Franconia Ski Club Collection.

219. Esther Serafini to Franconia Ski Club members, January 29, 1947, Franconia Ski Club Collection.

220. Franconia Ski Club, Minutes of Club Meeting, Meeting of November 22, 1939.

221. Clinton Underhill, Franconia Ski Club Social Committee Report, April 7, 1948, Franconia Ski Club Collection.

222. Joan Hannah, telephone interview with author, April 22, 2010.

223. Franconia Ski Club, Minutes of Club Meeting, Meeting of May 7, 1947.

224. Robert W. Edge, Memorandum on President's Cup, March 22, 1955, Franconia Ski Club Collection.

225. President's Cup Announcement, March 30, 1958, Franconia Ski Club Collection.

226. Gloria Chadwick bio, http://www.skihall.org/index.php?act=viewDoc&docId=11&id=63.

227. Charles Wellborn, *History of the 86th Mountain Infantry in Italy*, www.10thmtndivassoc.org/86thhistory.pdf, p. 23.

228. *Courier*, "Juniors Have Awards Banquet," March 8, 1956, 1.

229. Bill Flynn, "Ski Instructor Gets Lifetime Award," *Courier*, March 20, 1996.

230. *Courier*, "Franconia Ski Club Junior Racers to Compete at Whitefish, Montana," March 3, 1955.

231. Gilbert Oakes to William Carpenter, July 23, 1971, Franconia Ski Club Collection.

232. Lynn Bishop, personal interview with author, April 20, 2010.

233. Bill Husson, personal interview with author, April 21, 2010.

234. Anita Craven, "History of the Franconia Ski Club," www.franconiaskiclub.com/history.php.

235. Chet Thompson, telephone interview with author, October 25, 2010.

236. Trevor Hamilton, telephone interview by author, November 15, 2010.

THE 1967 WORLD CUP

237. Patrick Lang, "The FIS Alpine Ski World Cup," FIS, http://www.fisalpine.com/fis-info/world-cup-history.html.

238. Gordi Eaton, telephone interview by author, November 22, 2010.

239. Bob Beattie, telephone interview by author, November 22, 2010.

240. Ibid.

241. Robert Lindsey, "Eastern Inter-Club Ski League Celebrates 50 Years," EICSL publication, February 25, 2003, www.eicsl.org/50th-Anniversary-Book.pdf.

242. "Numerous Private Sources Contribute Equipment for Big Cannon Mountain Race," New Hampshire Division of Economic Development press release, February 17, 1967, NESM; "New Hampshire Pledges Support to Off-Year Olympic Ski Race at Cannon Mountain," New Hampshire Division of Economic Development press release, December 8, 1966, NESM.

243. Bob Craven, "Ski Tales from Earlier Days at Cannon—Memories of Bill Kempton and the Diehards," February 16, 2010.

244. Dr. J. Leland Sosman biography, U.S. National Ski Hall of Fame, http://www.skihall.org/index.php?act=viewDoc&docId=11&id=309.

245. Willy Schaeffler biography, U.S. National Ski Hall of Fame, http://www.skihall.org/index.php?act=viewDoc&docId=11&id=294.

246. Austin Macaulay, "Story of Cannon Mt. Racecourse," *North American Alpine Championships program*, 1967.

247. "Numerous Private Sources Contribute Equipment"; "Many Groups Preparing for World Ski Cup Race at Cannon Mountain in March," New Hampshire Division of Economic Development press release, January 24, 1967, NESM.

248. Gordi Eaton, telephone interview.

249. Rich Millen, personal interview by author, July 26, 2010.

250. "Leading International Alpine Skiers Accept Invitations for Cannon Mountain Race," New Hampshire Division of Economic Development press release, February 27, 1967, NESM.

251. Rich Millen, personal interview by author, July 26, 2010.

252. North American Alpine Championships program, March 10–12, 1967.

253. Ernie Roberts, "Huber Austria's Ski Hero Until Time Recheck Gives Killy Win," *Boston Globe*, March 12, 1967, 59.

254. *Courier*, "Official Race Results," March 16, 1967, 1B.

255. "IBM Computer to Score Results During North American Alpine Races at Cannon Mountain," New Hampshire Division of Economic Development press release, February 17, 1967, NESM.

256. Crossley, *Take My Picture*, 88.

257. Dick Hamilton, telephone interview by author, October 28, 2010.

258. Ralph H. "Deak" Morse, "Success Crowns Cannon Mt. Ski Racing Weekend," *Courier*, March 16, 1967, 1.

259. Dick Hamilton, telephone interview.

260. Jeff Leich, personal correspondence with author, March 26, 2011.

261. Gordi Eaton, telephone interview by author, November 22, 2010.

CANNON TRAILS AND THEIR STORIES

262. Selden Hannah, transcript of interview.

263. *New Hampshire Troubadour*, "How Our Ski Trails Were Cut," January 1934, 11.

264. Roger Peabody, transcript of interview by Harry Stearns, November 28, 1980, NESM.

265. F.C. Matzek, "Down the Snow Trails" column, *Providence Bulletin*, December 9, 1941.

266. Selden Hannah and Edward Blood, "Survey of Cannon Mountain Ski Trail system," NESM, 2001.164.002E.

267. Jere Peabody, personal interview by author, July 26, 2010.

268. Mickey Libby, personal interview by author, July 15, 2004.

269. Ibid.

270. Joan Hannah, telephone interview by author, October 18, 2010.

271. Bill Mead, e-mail message to author, February 2, 2011.

272. Joel Peabody, telephone interview with author, November 15, 2010.

273. Meghan McCarthy, "What's in a (Trail) Name? A Lifetime of Memories," *Courier*, December 10, 2003, 1C, 12C.

274. Joan Hannah, telephone interview by author, November 2, 2003.

275. Kathy McCarthy, personal interview by author, November 15, 2010.

276. Jere Peabody, e-mail to author, September 27, 2010.

CANNON RACERS, INNKEEPERS
AND MOUNTAIN MANAGERS

277. Harry Reid, personal interview by author, July 28, 2008.

278. Joan Hannah biography, U.S. National Ski Hall of Fame, http://www.skihall.org/index.php?act=viewDoc&docId=11&id=129.

279. Sel Hannah, transcript of interview.

280. Joan Hannah, personal interview by author, October 18, 2010.

281. "Sel Hannah: Skier, Farmer, Innkeeper, Pioneer in Ski Area Development," biographical notes from Sel Hannah's files, undated.

282. Gordi Eaton, telephone interview by author, November 22, 2010.

283. Miller with McEnany, *Bode*, 9.

284. Bode Miller biography, U.S. Ski Team, http://www.usskiteam.com/alpine/athletes/athlete?athleteId=1243.

285. Miller with McEnany, *Bode*, 38.

286. "Diana Golden Brosnihan—1963–2001," *New England Ski Museum Newsletter* (Summer 2001): 22–23.

287. Robert Sullivan, "To Race or Not to Race? At Inferno Time, That's the Enduring Question," *Sports Illustrated*, April 4, 1983, 120–22.

288. "Schmid-Sommer and Anderson crowned National Champions," USTSA website, http://www.ustsa.org/new-site/index.php?option=com_content&view=article&id=389:schmid-sommer-and-anderson-crowned-national-champions&catid=1:latest-news&Itemid=50.

289. John Jerome, "Where it All Began," *Skiing*, February 1977, 44–46.

290. Chuck Lovett, personal interview with author, January 14, 2011.

291. Joan Hannah, personal interview with author, April 22, 2010.

292. Nicolas Howe, "Franconia Then and Now," *Skiing*, January 1981, 53.

293. Joe Cushing, personal interview by author, May 10, 2010.

294 Jo Miller, telephone interview with author, February 15, 2011.

295. *93 Ski Week*, "Rich in Tradition, Cannon Maintains Dedicated Staff," 1975, 6–7; Jack Colby, "Tri-Generational Partnership Is Part of Cannon Mtn's History," *Courier*, September 1, 1999, 7.

296. Phil Gravink, telephone interview with author, May 31, 2005.

297. *Courier*, "Funeral Held Sunday for Newton Avery, Well Known Tramway Official," March 28, 1968, 5.

298. Bill Roy, telephone interview with author, September 20, 2010.

299. Ibid.

300. Dick Andross, telephone interview with author, March 10, 2011.

301. Bill Roy, telephone interview.

302. John DeVivo, email message to author, January 31, 2011.

Timeline of Cannon Events

303. Photocopy of "Statement by Commissioner Robb R. Thomson Regarding the Request for Proposals for Cannon Mountain and Mount Sunapee," April 29, 1998, Rich McLeod files.

BIBLIOGRAPHY

Books and Papers

Adler, Allen. *That Peckett Mystique*. Collected Papers of the 2002 International Ski History Congress. Park City, Utah.

Allen, E. John B. *From Skisport to Skiing: One Hundred Years of an American Sport, 1840–1940*. Amherst: University of Massachusetts Press, 1993.

Crossley, Dorothy I. *Take My Picture: Memoirs & Photographs of Skiing and Sailing*. Etna, NH: Durand Press, 2005.

Jay, John. *Ski Down the Years*. New York: Universal Publishing & Distribution Corporation, 1966.

Johnson Hancock, Frances Ann. *Saving the Great Stone Face*. Edited by Ruth Ayres-Givens. Canaan, NH: Phoenix Publishing, for Franconia Area Heritage Council, 1984.

Miller, Bode, with Jack McEnany. *Bode: Go Fast, Be Good, Have Fun*. New York: Villard, 2005.

von Pantz, Baron Hubert (as told to Eva C. Huvos). *No Risk, No Fun!* New York: Vantage Press, 1986.

Welch, Sarah. *A History of Franconia New Hampshire*. Littleton, NH: Courier Printing Company, 1972.

INTERVIEWS AND CORRESPONDENCE

Allen Adler
Greg Anthony
Bob Ball
Katharine Holman Bigelow
Lynn Bishop
Peg Branch
Phil Branch
Christina Valar Breen
Cameron Bright
Peter Clark
Kim Cowles
Dorothy Crossley
Joe Cushing
John DeVivo
Gordi Eaton
Jennifer Peabody Gaudette
Marcia Graham
Phil Gravink
Dick Hamilton
Trevor Hamilton
Joan Hannah
Gary Harwood
Bill Husson
Jeffrey Leich
Mickey Libby

Chuck Lovett
Ray Martin
Billy McCarthy
Kathy McCarthy
William "Red" McCarthy
Jack McGurin
Martha McLeod
Rich McLeod
Bill Mead
Rich Millen
Jo Miller
Bunny Nutter
Jere Peabody
Joel Peabody
Roger Peabody
Harry Reid
Wody Robertson
Bill Roy
Barbara Serafini
Chet Thompson
Susan Thompson
Paul Valar
Stefanie Valar
Bonnie Van Slyke

INTERVIEW AUDIOTAPES OR TRANSCRIPTS, BIOGRAPHICAL NOTES FROM THE NEW ENGLAND SKI MUSEUM COLLECTION

Norwood Ball
Kenneth Boothroyd
Shirley Campbell
Leah Cole

Selden Hannah
Roger Peabody
Paula Valar
Hubert von Pantz

OTHER SOURCES

Craven, Anita, comp. *Franconia Ski Club—Officers and History—The first 70 Years*. March 2003.

Enzo Serafini Collection (scrapbooks and clippings)

Franconia Ski Club Collection (historic correspondence, documents and clippings)

Hannah Family (notes and correspondence)

International Skiing History Association, "Timeline of Important Ski History Dates," www.skiinghistory.org/historicdates.html.

Marcia Graham (notes and correspondence re: Mittersill Association of Chalet Owners)

McLeod, Richard, comp. *The State Park System According to the Record by Law and Significant Event*. N.d.

New England Ski Museum, "Timeline of New Hampshire Downhill Skiing," www.nesm.org/timeline.html.

ABOUT THE AUTHOR

Meghan McCarthy McPhaul has been skiing at Cannon Mountain since she was a small child in the 1970s. After spending five years in the mountains of Colorado, she returned to the East and began a career as a small-town newspaper reporter, earning accolades and professional journalism awards while working on the side as a ski coach. She continues to write for local and regional publications, and her work has recently been included in two collections of essays: *Wildbranch: An*  *Anthology of Nature, Environmental, and Place-based Writing* and *Beyond the Notches: Stories of Place in New Hampshire's North Country*. For more information, visit www.meghanmcphaul.com.

Visit us at
www.historypress.net